Donna ☑ P9-AGO-687
(Oct 8, 1932 – Jan 14, 2008)

3/24/08
Linda Hannisdal

Merovingian
Military Organization
481–751

Merovingian
Military Organization
481-751

BERNARD S. BACHRACH

UNIVERSITY OF MINNESOTA PRESS
Minneapolis

© Copyright 1972 by the University of Minnesota.
All rights reserved.
Printed in the United States of America
at the University of Minnesota Printing Department, Minneapolis.
Published in the United Kingdom and India by the Oxford University
Press, London and Delhi, and in Canada
by the Copp Clark Publishing Co. Limited, Toronto

Library of Congress Catalog Card Number: 70-187164

ISBN 0-8166-0621-8

to

MY PARENTS

Preface

This monograph is a study of the military institutions which flourished in Gaul from the accession of Clovis in 481 to the deposition of Childeric III in 751. Previous work on this subject has been limited to specialized articles and sections of general works. These efforts have been based upon a small selection of the available evidence and have resulted in a distorted understanding of Merovingian military organization. In the present study the use of all the significant sources has made it possible to ascertain that there was great diversity as well as substantial change in the military institutions of Merovingian Gaul.

A secondary aim of this book has been to investigate the relation of the organization of the armed forces to the exercise of political power during this period. Although it would be a distortion of the situation to assert that military institutions were the only forces which impinged upon political life in early medieval Gaul, it would be equally false to argue that such institutions were not of great importance in the political sphere. It is worth recalling here the words of the Roman Emperor Septimius Severus that the army should be showered with gold and all else should be regarded as of secondary consequence. For it cannot be ignored that Merovingian society and its military organization grew up among the ruins of the Roman Empire, that they reflect *Romania* more than *Germania*.

PREFACE

Through their encouragement and advice many people have made my work on this book both easier and more pleasant. I would like, however, to make special mention of Professors F. L. Ganshof, Walter Goffart, R. S. Hoyt, and Bryce Lyon who read the entire manuscript at one or another stage in its history and provided valuable criticism. It would be less than fair, in addition, if I did not share with my wife Debby the credit for bringing this work to completion. Despite her obligations as wife, mother, and scholar she found the time to read proofs and help with the compilation of the index. Lastly, it gives me pleasure to note that this study was awarded the McKnight Foundation Prize in European History in 1968.

BERNARD S. BACHRACH

November 3, 1971
St. Paul, Minn.

Contents

Abbreviations

AHR	*American Historical Review*
BEC	*Bibliothèque de l'École des Chartes*
CRAI	*Comptes Rendus de l'Académie des Inscriptions et Belles-Lettres*
HZ	*Historische Zeitschrift*
JRS	*Journal of Roman Studies*
MA	*Le Moyen Âge*
MGH	*Monumenta Germaniae Historica*
AA	*Auctores Antiquissimi*
Ep	*Epistolae*
LL	*Leges*
SS	*Scriptores*
SSRL	*Scriptores Rerum Langobardicarum*
SSRM	*Scriptores Rerum Merovingicarum*
MIÖG	*Mitteilungen des Instituts für Österreichische Geschichtsforschung*
REA	*Revue des Études Anciennes*
RH	*Revue Historique*
RPBH	*Revue Belge de Philologie et d'Histoire*
ZRG	*Zeitschrift der Savigny-Stiftung für Rechtsgeschichte*

Merovingian
Military Organization
481–751

Clovis: 481–511

AFTER the death of Aetius in 454, imperial power in Gaul rapidly disintegrated and the wealth of this Roman province was controlled by those who were able to muster the armed force necessary to keep it. By 481 the two peoples competing for predominance in this territory were the Visigoths in southwestern Gaul and the Burgundians in the southeast. Among the lesser groups contending for power were the *Armorici* (a loose confederation of Gallo-Romans, Britons, Alans, and erstwhile imperial soldiers with their families), who lived in the area between the Seine and the Loire. To the north, between the Seine and the Somme, was Syagrius's Roman kingdom of Soissons and to the east along the upper Rhine were settlements of Alamans. North of these was a small band of Thuringians. The remainder of the Rhineland and the area to the west were ruled by Frankish *reguli* or chieftains, who, with their warbands, were settled around Tournai, Cambrai, Cologne, and the other cities of the region.[1]

It was one of these *reguli*, Clovis, the ruler of Tournai, who, starting with a small warband, was to gain the support of an armed force large enough to take control of most of Gaul. The

---

[1] Procopius, *H.W.*, V, xii, 8ff; Jordanes, *Getica*, LV. On this see Bernard S. Bachrach, "Procopius and the Chronology of Clovis's Reign," *Viator*, I (1970), 21–25, and cf. J. M. Wallace-Hadrill, *The Long-Haired Kings* (London, 1962), p. 161.

Merovingian military began with Clovis's warband and grew with his and his descendants' successes.

In 481, at about the age of sixteen, Clovis succeeded his father, Childeric, as ruler of Tournai. He thereby came into possession of the imperial installations including the fisc, and took command of his father's warband, which probably amounted to no more than 400 or 500 warriors. Among Childeric's followers a prominent role seems to have been played by a Hun named Wiomad, which suggests that other than Frankish elements may have served Clovis.[2]

In 486 Clovis began his efforts to expand the kingdom when he allied with his relative Ragnachar, the ruler of Cambrai, to attack Syagrius of Soissons. As the battle progressed, Syagrius, seeing his troops defeated, fled south to Toulouse and sought refuge with the Visigothic king, Alaric II. The latter, however, handed Syagrius over to Clovis who liquidated him.[3] This victory over Syagrius gave Clovis control of the *civitas* of Soissons with its fortifications and arms factory, the existence of which may well have been partly responsible for the Roman ruler's choosing it as a headquarters initially.[4] Other cities within the area between the Somme and the Seine did not immediately accept Clovis's rule. He laid siege to Verdun and it finally surrendered. Paris was also besieged, but its conquest presented Clovis with a knotty tactical problem. Though the extant sources concerning the siege of Paris are admittedly of limited value, they suggest that it took Clovis several years, perhaps as many as five, to gain control of the city, or more precisely of the fortress. The Ile de la Cité seems to have been supplied by boat, and Clovis, at that point in his career, did not have at his disposal naval forces of sufficient strength to halt such activity.[5]

[2] Though much has been written since its appearance, G. Kurth's *Clovis*, 2nd ed., 2 vols. (Paris, 1901), remains fundamental. Wallace-Hadrill's *Long-Haired Kings*, pp. 159–185, is of special worth. On the size of Clovis's forces see Bachrach, "Clovis's Reign," p. 28, and the literature cited there.

[3] Gregory, *Hist.*, II, 27.

[4] Wallace-Hadrill, *Long-Haired Kings*, p. 159.

[5] *V. Genov.*, ch. 35: "Factum est autem, ut Genovefa in Arciacinse opido navali effectione ad conparandam annonam profiscisceretur"; and ch. 40:

CLOVIS

It is not known precisely at what date Clovis finally secured control of the entire Roman kingdom of Soissons. But probably by 491, when he directed his attention elsewhere, not only had the Roman units which had served Syagrius been integrated into his following, but the military colonists (*laeti*) settled in that area under the empire had also come under his control.[6] A relatively large amount of evidence has survived concerning the *laeti*. In Belgica II between Rheims and Amiens there was a Sarmatian military colony. From place names which are still extant, indicating a long-lasting habitation, it can be ascertained that there were settlements within this colony at Sermiers (Marne), Sermaize les Bains (Marne), Sermoise (Aisne), and Sermaise (Oise).[7] In the colony established between Paris and Saint-Moré (Yonne), two other settlements can be identified — Sermaise (Seine-et-Oise) and Sermaise (Seine-et-Marne).[8] There were Alaman military colonies at Rheims and Senlis.[9] All these military colonies were *corpora publica* under the empire and it seems reasonable to assume that Clovis gained control of them in the same manner as he took over the remains of the imperial fisc.[10]

When Clovis turned his attention from the area between the Somme and the Seine in about 491, he moved against a small group of Thuringians settled in eastern Gaul north of the Burgundians. Nothing is known about this campaign except that Clovis was victorious. It can be assumed, however, that as a result of this campaign his interests were more likely to come into

"Regressa itaque Parissius, unicuique, prout opus fuit, frugem dispersit." *V. Maximini*, p. 393. On these see Kurth, *Clovis*, I, 245–248.

[6] Bachrach, "Clovis's Reign," pp. 23–24. Cf. Wallace-Hadrill, *Long-Haired Kings*, pp. 164–165.

[7] *Notitia Dignitatum, oc.*, XLII, 67: "Praefectus Sarmatarum gentilium, inter Renos et Tambianos provinciae Belgicae secundae." A. Longnon, *Les noms de lieu de la France* (Paris, 1920), no. 528, for Sermiers, and no. 532, for Sarmaize les Bains, Sermoise, and Sermaise.

[8] *Notitia Dignitatum, oc.*, XLII, 66: "Praefectus Sarmatarum gentilium, a Chora Parisios usque." Longnon, *Les noms*, no. 532, for both Sermaises.

[9] *Notitia Dignitatum, oc.*, XLII, 42.

[10] A. H. M. Jones, *The Later Roman Empire* (Norman, Okla., 1964), I, 620; A. Grenier, *Manuel d'archéologie Gallo-Romain* (Paris, 1931), V, 398ff.

direct conflict with those of the Alamans along the middle Rhine and those of the Burgundians to the south.[11]

In 496 the Alamans moved into Frankish territory, and the various Salian and Ripuarian *reguli* seem to have joined their followings under Clovis's leadership to stop this invasion. At Tolbiac, some thirty miles south of Cologne, the two armies met and the Alamans were defeated. Though Tolbiac was a formidable fortress, it seems that this battle, unlike several of Clovis's previous actions, did not involve siege warfare. The exact nature of the battle, however, aside from its outcome, remains unknown.[12]

Clovis's victory at Tolbiac was of much greater consequence than merely the turning back of an enemy invasion; his adherence to Christianity and subsequent baptism were by and large directly related to this campaign. According to Gregory of Tours's account, Clovis seems to have undergone a religious experience: the Alamans were treating Clovis's forces roughly and he asked the Christian God for help, promising in effect that if his enemy were defeated he would become a Christian.[13]

Although it is not impossible that Clovis underwent a religious experience, it may be suggested that the interpretation of Clovis's postvictory baptism by Gregory or those he used as his sources resulted more from sincere wish fulfillment than from solid evidence. The political and military realities of Clovis's situation and his personality (even as depicted by Gregory) would reasonably lead us to conclude that the Frankish chief found motivation for his actions in other than spiritual demands. Clovis is known to have believed that if he were baptized he would lose the support of many of his pagan followers. To have been baptized in spite of this implies strong motivation indeed.[14]

[11]Bachrach, "Clovis's Reign," p. 21. Cf. Kurth, *Clovis*, I, 266ff.

[12] Gregory, *Hist.*, II, 30. The date of the battle of Tolbiac and Clovis's baptism, which seems to be intimately connected with it, is a major problem in the chronology of Clovis's reign. On this see Bachrach, "Clovis's Reign," p. 27, and the bibliography cited there.

[13] Gregory, *Hist.*, II, 30.

[14] *Ibid.*, II, 31: "At ille [Clovis] ait: 'Libenter te, sanctissime pater, audiebam; set restat unam, quod populus, qui me sequitur, non patitur reliquere deus suos; sed vado et loquor eius iuxta verbum tuum.'"

CLOVIS

It may be hypothesized that Clovis accepted Christianity and attempted to impose it upon his pagan followers to ensure the support of the Christian Gallo-Romans, especially the lay and ecclesiastical magnates who controlled great wealth and power. It should be remembered that the Alamans, Clovis's enemies, were pagans like the Franks and that the Gallo-Romans, while surely hostile to Arian barbarians like the Visigoths, would find little difference between one pagan group and another.

Shortly after Clovis had come to power, he had received a letter from Remigius, bishop of Rheims, indicating to the young king that he would find it advantageous to have the support of the Gallo-Roman church. The bishop's letter even implied that Clovis should show deference to the bishops and ask their advice; a meeting of minds between the young ruler and the influential churchmen, wrote Remigius, would assure a prosperous reign. This letter may be regarded as more a veiled threat than a humble request to a pagan ruler for religious toleration, for the Gallo-Roman church was the powerful leader of the Christian community and the bishops, many of whom were from old and established families, were not to be slighted.[15] Men like Hilarius, bishop of Arles, who during the previous generation had led his band of armed retainers contrary to imperial proscription, could be either useful supporters or very dangerous enemies of a young and untried barbarian monarch. Bishops Quintianus of Rodez, Volusianus of Tours, Aprunculus of Langres, and Verus of Tours had caused so much trouble for the Visigothic and Burgundian leaders that ultimately they had to be driven from their sees. The details of their opposition to such barbarians as the Visigoths and Burgundians are unknown, but it is doubtful that they went as far as Bishop Galactorius of Béarn who was killed while leading an armed force to support Clovis against the Visigoths. On the other hand, these bishops may have been more like Cautinus of Auvergne who used his armed supporters to pillage his neighbors.[16]

[15] *MGH epist. Merov. et Karl.*, II, 113.

[16] *N. Val.*, 17, 1, for Hilarius and his armed followers. Gregory, *Hist.*, II, 36, for Quintianus; II, 22, and X, 31, for Volusianus; II, 23, for Aprunculus;

Whether or not Clovis had made overtures to the bishops as a result of Remigius's letter is not known. But he apparently did not enjoy the support of the ecclesiastical magnates in 486 when he went to battle against Syagrius. Clovis had followed up his victory in Soissons by pillaging Syagrius's kingdom, including the churches. The booty had not even been divided when Clovis received a messenger from Remigius requesting that the items taken from the church at Rheims, especially a very valuable ewer, be returned. Clovis did return at least the ewer, and it seems somewhat likely that this gesture marked an effort by the Frankish king to establish or reestablish cordial relations with the powerful bishop of Rheims.[17]

By the time of the battle of Tolbiac (ten years after the pillaging of Syagrius's kingdom), Clovis had made some further concessions to the Gallo-Roman power structure: he had taken a Christian wife and had permitted his children to be baptized. These might not have been regarded as sufficient, however, and he realized the wisdom of Remigius's earlier admonitions that the support of the churchmen would be advantageous. Clovis now was in a difficult position: with the help of the Gallo-Roman magnates he could rule Gaul; without it he was just another *regulus*. The Alaman invasion presented a choice to the Gallo-Romans and they were in a position to demand a large price for their support; presumably they did. Additional support for this interpretation is lent by a story preserved in the *Liber Historiae Francorum* in which Aurelianus, a Gallo-Roman who served Clovis in a military capacity, is credited with suggesting

---

X, 31, for Verus; and V. *Galact.*, p. 434, for Galactorius. For discussions of this see Kurth, *Clovis*, II, 84–85, and Samuel Dill, *Roman Society in Gaul in the Merovingian Age* (London, 1926), p. 95. Cf. E. A. Thompson, *The Goths in Spain* (Oxford, 1969), pp. 26–27. For Cautinus see Gregory, *Hist.*, IV, 12, and the discussion below in ch. 2, n. 23.

[17] Gregory, *Hist.*, II, 27. The legend of the recalcitrant warrior and the ewer which is interwoven into this episode may perhaps symbolize a factional struggle among Clovis's followers concerning the church, a struggle which seems to have had later repercussions. See G. Kurth, *Histoire poétique des Mérovingiens* (Paris, 1893), pp. 223–224, and Kurth, *Clovis*, I, 244.

to the Frankish chief at Tolbiac that his military situation would prosper if he became a Christian.[18]

In any event, Clovis judged correctly when he concluded that his baptism would not be supported fully by his pagan followers. Of the 6000 or so Frankish warriors who formed the warbands of the *reguli*, only some 3000 followed Clovis to the baptismal font. The other half joined with Ragnachar, the *regulus* of Cambrai, who remained a pagan.[19] Although Clovis had probably lost about one half of his Frankish followers, he was still able, in the years following his baptism, to continue his military activities. In 500 or 501 relations between Godigisel and Gundobad, the Burgundian kings, became strained and the former asked Clovis for military aid against the latter. In return for this aid, Godigisel agreed to give Clovis a yearly payment as well as a portion of the Burgundian kingdom. When Clovis's army entered Burgundy, Gundobad told his brother of the invasion and asked him to take the field against the Frankish ruler. To Gundobad's surprise, when the three armies arrived outside of Dijon, he was attacked by his brother as well as by Clovis. Though his army was defeated, Gundobad managed to escape to the fortified city of Avignon.[20]

After this battle, Godigisel retired to Vienne, but Clovis led his followers against Gundobad at Avignon and laid siege to the fortress, presumably with the siege engines (*instrumenta belli*) with which he had begun the campaign. Clovis's men devastated the area around the city, pillaging and burning everything within reach. But a certain Aridius, a Gallo-Roman magnate in the service of Gundobad, gained Clovis's confidence and convinced

---

[18] *L.H.F.*, ch. 15. For further discussion of Aurelianus see n. 41 below. Cf. Wallace-Hadrill, *Long-Haired Kings*, p. 168.

[19] *V. Remigii*, ch. 15: "Multi denique de Francorum exercitu, necdum ad fidem conversi, sum regis parente Ragnario ultra Sumnam fluvium aliquandiu deguerunt, donec, Christi gratia cooperante, gloriosis potitus victoriis, eundem Ragnarium, flagitiis turpitudinum inservientem, vinctum a Francis sibi traditum, rex Hludowicus occidit et omnem Francorum populum per beatum Remigium ad fidem converti et baptizari obtinuit." Gregory, *Hist.*, II, 31: "De exercito vero eius baptizati sunt amplius tria milia." Dill, *Merovingian Age*, pp. 77, 80; Bachrach, "Clovis's Reign," pp. 27–28; and Wallace-Hadrill, *Long-Haired Kings*, p. 170.

[20] Gregory, *Hist.*, II, 32.

him that Avignon could not be taken. Peace was then negotiated; Gundobad agreed to pay Clovis a yearly tribute and the latter returned home with his followers.[21]

A year or two later Clovis led his forces into Armorica, the area between the Seine and the Loire. Unlike his previous raids into this area (which may have taken place during the late 480s), this campaign seems to have been aimed at subjugating the *Armorici*. Clovis's forces, however, were defeated. Yet the *Armorici*, who, like Clovis, were Christians, desired cordial relations with him to counterbalance the hostile Arian Visigoths who coveted the land north of the Loire. Therefore, an accord was arranged by which Clovis came to rule the various peoples of Armorica and the military strength of the area was integrated into the Merovingian military.[22]

Among the inhabitants of the *Tractus Armoricani* who joined Clovis's military following were the Alans, who dominated the Orleanais and the area to the north, Gallo-Roman magnates and their adherents, former Roman soldiers and their descendants who had maintained their military organization, Bretons, imperial military colonists (*laeti*) from Chartres, Bayeux, Coutance, Le Mans, and Rennes, and Rome's Saxon allies of Bayeux.[23] Not long after acquiring the support of the inhabitants of Armorica, Clovis again went to war against the Alamans, who had regained some of their previous strength during the decade of disunity among the Frankish *reguli* following Clovis's baptism. No details of the campaign survive other than the fact that Clovis was victorious. After this victory some of the defeated Alamans fled to the lands of Theodoric the Great, while others remained

[21] *Ibid.*

[22] Procopius *H.W.*, V, xii, 13ff. On this text see Bachrach, "Clovis's Reign," pp. 28–29.

[23] Procopius, *H.W.*, V, xii, 16ff. On the Alans see Bernard S. Bachrach, "The Origin of Armorican Chivalry," *Technology and Culture*, X (1969), 166–171, and "The Alans in Gaul," *Traditio*, XXIII (1967), 476–489. For the *laeti* see *Notitia Dignitatum, oc.*, XLII, 33, 34, 35, 36. On the survival of Roman units in Gaul see Bernard S. Bachrach, "A Note on Alites," *Byzantinische Zeitschrift*, LXI (1968), 35.

under Merovingian domination and ultimately served in the armed forces of Clovis's successors.[24]

In 507, after having obtained the consent of his magnates, Clovis launched an invasion of the Visigothic kingdom. The Merovingian king made a concerted effort to keep the support of the church by forbidding his troops to plunder its possessions. One of Clovis's orders restricted his men to the use of only grass and water in provisioning their mounts on the church lands they traversed. Clovis's horsemen generally seem to have abided by this order, although present knowledge of it may well have survived because of the drastic manner in which a violator was punished. Much to the joy of such clerical observers as Gregory of Tours, Clovis enforced this order by killing the man who violated it with his own hand.[25]

Though Clovis's advance south was slowed somewhat by the rain-swollen Vienne River, his forces reached the Poitiers area and engaged the Visigoths at Vouillé, a plain to the south of the city on the Roman road to Nantes. Clovis's archers and spear throwers, apparently deployed at the rear of his formation, showered the Goths with missiles from a distance. While this barrage battered the enemy, other elements of Clovis's force advanced and engaged the Goths in hand-to-hand combat. Clovis is alleged to have killed Alaric, the Visigothic king, in single combat, and only just escaped death himself when the speed of his horse and the strength of his cuirass combined to thwart the efforts of two Gothic warriors. The Visigoths turned and fled and Clovis's forces won the day.[26]

Clovis followed up his triumph over the Visigoths by sending his son Theuderic to seize the cities held by the Goths in the south of Gaul. Albi, Rodez, and Clermont all fell under Mero-

[24] F. Lot, "La victoire sur les Alamans et la conversion de Clovis," RBPH, XVII (1938), 63–69, and Bachrach, "Clovis's Reign," p. 30. Cf. A. Van de Vyver, "L'unique victoire contre les Alamans et la conversion de Clovis en 506," RBPH, XVII (1938), 793–813.

[25] Gregory, Hist., II, 37: ". . . ut nullus de regione illa aliud, quam herbarum alimenta aquamque praesumeret."

[26] Ibid.: "Chlodovechus rex cum Alarico rege Gothorum in compo Vogladense decimo ab urbe Pictava milario convenit, et confligentibus his eminus, resistunt comminus illi."

vingian control, and Gregory of Tours somewhat optimistically remarks that the whole country from the Gothic to the Burgundian border was brought under Clovis's domination.[27] The Merovingian advance, however, did not go unchallenged. A force of Merovingians and Burgundians, which besieged Arles for several months, was driven off by an Ostrogothic army and suffered great losses.[28] Clovis took Bordeaux in 507 and wintered in the city. During the next year he captured Toulouse and the Visigothic treasure stored there. While besieging Carcassonne, however, Clovis's army was driven off by Ostrogothic troops. Clovis then moved north and took Angoulême, forcing out the Gothic garrison. To secure his conquests, Clovis established garrisons throughout the newly won territories; the sources make specific mention of garrisons at Toulouse, Rodez, Saintes, and Bordeaux.[29]

Although Clovis's control of the Visigothic kingdom in Gaul was challenged and he lost Septimania, he was able to secure the more northerly areas. The Taifal and Sarmatian *laeti* in the Poitiers area, as well as the Sarmatians in the Rodez-Velay region, joined the ranks of the Merovingian military. The Alaman *laeti* who garrisoned fortresses in the Auvergne, and some of the Alans living in the area between the Mediterranean and Toulouse may probably also be counted as additions to Clovis's forces.[30]

[27] *Ibid.*

[28] *V. Caes.*, ch. 28, and Jordanes, *Getica*, LVIII.

[29] Gregory, *Hist.*, II, 37; Procopius, *H.W.*, V, xii, 41ff; Isid., *Hist. Goth.*, 281–282: "Alaricus . . . tandem provocatus a Francis in regione Pictavensis urbis proelio initio extinguitur eoque interfecto regnum Tolosanum occupantibus Francis destruitur"; *L.H.F.*, ch. 17: "In Sanctonico vel Burdigalinse Francos precepit manere ad gothorum gentem delendam"; *Gesta Francorum*, col. 414–415: "His igitur ita patratis, cum ad solum proprium redire deliberaret, electos milites atque fortissimos cum parvulis atque mulieribus ad pervasas civitates custodiendas et ad reprimendam Gothorum saeviatiam dereliquit, et immensis muneribus ampliavit." For a discussion of the garrisons and a defense of the *Gesta* on this point see Wallace-Hadrill, *Long-Haired Kings*, p. 31, n. 2. To the above references add *V. Dalmat.*, ch. 6: "Cumque ad illum devotissimus ardue festinaret, in Ultralegeretanis partibus quodam loco, ubi aliqua, ut dicam prope legio Bretonum manet. . . ." See also n. 23 above and n. 38 below.

[30] *Notitia Dignitatum*, *oc.*, XLII, 65: "Praefectus Sarmatarum et Taifalorum gentilium, Pictavis [in Galia]." The area around Poitiers was so thor-

CLOVIS

In the decade after his baptism, Clovis vastly increased the size of his kingdom, added huge quantities of wealth to his treasury, and greatly augmented his military establishment. He then turned his attention, in what were to be the last years of his life, to the Frankish warbands which had deserted him in 496 to follow Ragnachar. Largely through bribery, assassination, and murder, Clovis was able to eliminate the *reguli* and take over their warbands. Among the many with whom he dealt (all seemingly his relatives) was Sigibert of Cologne who was murdered by his own son at Clovis's instigation. Clovis then had the son murdered. Chararic and his son were captured and executed soon after. Ragnachar and his brothers Riccar and Rignomer seem to have been the last of the *reguli* to fall. Clovis bribed their *leudes*, who consequently refused to fight, then captured their former lords; the brothers were handed over to Clovis who killed them. With Ragnachar's death the remaining warbands joined Clovis and received baptism.[31]

Concerning Clovis's following and the warriors of the other *reguli* little is known. Whether the members of these forces may be identified with the *antrustiones* is a matter of conjecture, though surely at least some of them were bound by the special oath of those in the *trustis*.[32] The *leudes* of a *regulus* were also part of his following. The important role played by Ragnachar's *leudes* in his fall from power suggests that they were not simple warriors, but perhaps minor leaders with small warbands of their own.

Though the nature of these warbands, of whatever size, still generally remains obscure, some light may be thrown on the

---

oughly influenced by the Taifals that it was called Thifilia during the sixth century. Gregory, *V.P.*, XV, 1: "Igitur beatus Senoch, gente Theiphalus, Pictavi pagus, quem Theiphaliam vocant oriundus fuit." A. Longnon, *Géographie de la Gaule au VIᵉ siècle* (Paris, 1878), p. 176, and Grenier, *Manuel d'archéologie*, V, 398. For Alaman *laeti* see n. 37 below, and for the Alans see n. 22 above.

[31] Gregory, *Hist.*, II, 40, 41, 42. See Bachrach, "Clovis's Reign," p. 30, and cf. Kurth, *Clovis*, I, 266–268.

[32] M. Deloche, *La trustis et l'antrustion royal sous les deux premières races* (Paris, 1873), though old and in need of revision, is still the most complete work on the subject.

equestrian nature of Frankish arms. The Roman empire had found the Franks to be able horsemen and therefore, under its pragmatic policy of using barbarians for the kind of service to which they were best suited, recruited them for cavalry regiments. Of the four manifestly Frankish units listed in the *Notitia Dignitatum*, which was current during the first third of the fifth century, if indeed not later, all were mounted.[33] Childeric himself was so equestrian-oriented that he had the head of his warhorse entombed with him at Tournai.[34] And Clovis's own order regarding the taking of food and water for mounts immediately before the Visigothic campaign in 507 and the execution of an unimportant Frank for its violation illlustrate the significance of horsemen in his army. The importance of horses to the Franks is clearly indicated by the frequent legislation regarding them, even in the earliest compilation of the *Lex Salica,* about 510.[35] It may even be speculated that at the time of Clovis's baptism Bishop Remigius referred to Clovis as a "Sicamber" because the Frankish leader and his followers brought to mind their putative ancestors, the *Sicambri,* whose 2000 horsemen had gained some fame from Caesar's writings. Had Remigius been impressed with the pedestrian, rather than the equestrian, nature of the Franks' military mien, he probably would have called Clovis a Chatuarian, evoking memories of another putative ancestral tribe whose forte was infantry.[36]

Among the *laeti* added to Clovis's fighting forces horsemen were also prominent. Sarmatians, Taifals, and Alamans had a long history as mounted warriors and the empire had responded predictably by recruiting them for cavalry regiments; in fact, all Taifal and Sarmatian units in the Roman army were cavalry. Clovis acquired *laeti* as his followers and even admitted them to his personal following as *antrustiones.*[37]

[33] *Notitia Dignitatum, or.,* XXI, 51; XXXII, 35; XXXVI, 33; XXXI, 67.
[34] Cf. Wallace-Hadrill, *Long-Haired Kings,* p. 162.
[35] See Appendix, n. 27.
[36] Gregory, *Hist.,* II, 31: " '. . . Mitis depone colla, Sigamber; adora quod incendisti, incendi quod adorasti.' " Caesar, *B.G.,* VI, 35: "Cogunt equitum duo milia sugambir. . . ." and Tacitus, *Germ.,* 30: ". . . omne robur in pedite. . . ." concerning the Chatti.
[37] *Notitia Dignitatum, oc.,* VI, 59; XL, 54; *or.,* V, 31; XXVIII, 26; XXXII,

CLOVIS

The remains of the formal units of the Roman military also swelled the ranks of Clovis's army. Many of these infantry and cavalry regiments apparently maintained their military organization and training after the collapse of the empire, even handing down their customs to their descendants.[38] Surely only a small percentage of the descendants of the approximately 70,000 troops listed as being stationed in Gaul about 408 continued the military heritage of their ancestors to the end of the fifth century and beyond, but nevertheless some did. Of these the horsemen, of which there were about 6000, were probably the most useful to Clovis since they were elite troops. At least some of them possibly continued to function as they seem to have done in Britain.[39]

Among Rome's former allies in Gaul who came under Merovingian control were the Saxons of Bayeux, the Alans of Armorica, and some of those Alans established in the area between Toulouse and the Mediterranean. The Saxons may well have been primarily seamen, but the Alans were renowned as horsemen. The latter's equestrian tactics, common to the steppes, continued to influence military development in Armorica well into the Middle Ages.[40]

Another element in the Merovingian military was the armed forces of the Gallo-Roman magnates. As early as 493, Clovis could count on the support of a Gallo-Roman magnate like Aurelianus, who led his band in Clovis's service and who was given Melun as a reward for his loyalty.[41] Although the sources are

36; XXXIII, 31. *Lex Sal.*, XLII, 1: ". . . si in truste dominica fuerit iuratus ille qui occisus, LXXIIM denarios . . . culpabilis. . . ." Also 4: "De Romanis vero occisis vel letis [et pueris] haec lex [superius conprachensa ex] medietate solvatur."

[38] Procopius, *H.W.*, V, xii, 16ff. Bachrach, "Alites," p. 35.

[39] J. B. Bury, "The Notitia Dignitatum," *JRS*, X (1920), 146; Jones, *Later Roman Empire*, I, 619; II, 1449–1450. R. G. Collingwood and J. N. L. Myres, *Roman Britain*, 2nd ed. (Oxford, 1937), pp. 320ff.

[40] Bernard S. Bachrach, "The Feigned Retreat at Hastings," *Mediaeval Studies*, XXXIII (1971), 264–267, and Bachrach, "Armorican Chivalry," pp. 166–171.

[41] *L.H.F.*, chs. 11, 12, 14, 15. I cannot agree with Kurth, *Clovis*, II, 156, that Aurelianus is a legendary figure. Support for his historical existence may be found in K. F. Stroheker's *Der senatorische Adel in spätantiken Gallien*

extremely limited, it does seem reasonable to conclude that many such lay magnates joined Clovis during his successful career. It would be difficult to explain their failure to do so in light of the support Clovis received from the ecclesiastical magnates, the Roman lawyers who helped in drawing up *Lex Salica*, and the bureaucrats who operated his chancery.[42]

The magnates and their armed retainers had long played a role throughout the empire, and Rome had an ambivalent attitude toward the keeping of armed followers by these powerful men. Rome recognized that such groups served her own interests when used for the suppression of banditry and for the thwarting of barbarian raids, but she was equally aware that the magnates tended to utilize their armed retainers to help them gain control of large areas and to make the populations subject to private jurisdictions.[43] In Gaul there were Gallo-Roman magnates like Ecdicius, the brother-in-law of Sidonius Apollinaris, who raised a band of horsemen supported by his own funds and led it against the Visigoths.[44] Another such magnate was Titus; his activities as the leader of a band of *buccellarii* in Gaul gained the notice of the Emperor Leo, who was so impressed that he invited him to come to the East and gave him the title of *comes*.[45] Sidonius, in encouraging Eutropius to take a more active part in political affairs, listed his friend's qualifications for such action: an abundance of horses, armor, clothing, money,

---

(Tübingen, 1946), which lists four Aureliani (numbers 46–49), any of whom might be identified with Clovis's follower.

[42] Wallace-Hadrill, *Long-Haired Kings*, pp. 177ff.

[43] R. MacMullen, *Soldiers and Civilians in the Later Roman Empire* (Cambridge, Mass., 1963), ch. VI. *C. Th.*, 7.18.14; 9.14.2; *N. Val.*, 91. While many edicts in the *Theodosian Code* are specifically issued for a particular area, the conditions with which they deal may well have been more widespread at any given time. See Bernard S. Bachrach, "Was There Feudalism in Byzantine Egypt?" *Journal of the American Research Center in Egypt*, VI (1967), 163–166.

[44] Sidonius Apollinaris, *ep*. III, iii, 3, 5, 7: ". . . cum interiectis aequoribus in adversum perambulatis et vix duodeviginti equitum sodalitate comitatus aliquot milia Gothorum. . . ." Also, "taceo deinceps collegisse te privatis viribus publici exercitus speciem parvis extrinsecus maiorum opibus adiutum et infreniores hostium ante discursus castigatis cohercuisse populatibus."

[45] *V. Danielis*, ch. 60. See on this text Jones, *Later Roman Empire*, I, 666.

and retainers.[46] With such assets, and protected in his fortified villa, the Gallo-Roman magnate was a formidable figure in local affairs as well as on the battlefield.[47] With the support of this class of men and their followers, Clovis could provide professional fighting men for local defense and for the preservation of law and order as the empire had done before him. For they were an important element in the development of royal power.

The heterogeneous nature of the Merovingian military — warbands of the *reguli*, armed followings of the magnates, descendants of Roman soldiers who preserved their military customs, *laeti*, and Rome's barbarian allies — gave Clovis an experienced professional fighting force which could campaign throughout the year and was not restricted by the demands of agricultural labor as a part-time army of warrior-farmers would be. With a substantial mounted force of Alans, Sarmatians, Taifals, and some Franks and Alamans, Clovis's troops could successfully fight hand to hand against the Visigothic cavalry. His archers and spear throwers, probably drawn from erstwhile Roman units and from his own Franks, provided firepower on the field.[48] In siege warfare, undertaken by Clovis's forces on numerous occasions — at Verdun, Paris, Avignon, Arles, Carcassonne, and Angoulême — siege engines and other apparatus were probably employed.

Not only did Clovis's troops have the offensive capability to fight effectively on the open field as well as against fortified positions, but they also had the organizational flexibility both to fight year-round campaigns and to serve as garrisons in the many surviving fortified cities and *castra* in Gaul.[49] It can therefore be concluded that Clovis resuscitated the remains of the imperial military in Gaul and created the Merovingian military.

[46] Sidonius Apollinaris, *ep.* I, 6, 2: ". . . dein quod equis armis, veste sumptu famulicio instructus solum. . . ."

[47] MacMullen, *Soldiers and Civilians*, pp. 143, 147, and C. Jullian, *Histoire de la Gaule Romaine* (Paris, 1928), VIII, 139ff especially 141. MacMullen, p. 147, n. 101, feels that some of the fortified villas identified by Jullian are dubious.

[48] *Notitia Dignitatum, oc.*, VII, 75, and Gregory, *Hist.*, II, 9: ". . . sagittas turmentorum ritu effundere inlitas herbarum venensis. . . ."

[49] R. M. Butler, "Late Roman Town Walls in Gaul," *The Archaeological Journal*, CXVI (1959), 48–50.

CHAPTER II

The Sons
of Clovis: 511–561

W HEN Clovis died in 511, his kingdom was divided among his
    four sons, Theuderic, Childebert, Chlodomer, and Chlotar.
The first military encounter in which the Merovingian kings engaged after their father's death (at least the first of which some
record has survived) was against a force of Danish raiders who
invaded northern Gaul about 515. The Danes had come by sea
and had carried out a successful raid in which they acquired a
good deal of loot. The main force had returned to the ships and
only their king, Chlochiliach, remained on land, presumably
with a small group of his armed followers. Gregory of Tours
notes that Theudebert, having been sent by his father, Theuderic,
to repel the invaders, met them in a sea battle, defeated them
decisively, killed Chlochiliach, and recovered the booty from
the enemy ships.[1]

Several points are worth noting about this encounter. King
Theuderic, or at least his son Theudebert, had at his disposal
ships capable of engaging in sea warfare and men with the ability
to defeat a seagoing people at their own game. Also, Theudebert's
troops are described by Gregory as being a *validus exercitus* or

[1] Gregory, *Hist.*, III, 3: "Quod cum Theodorico nuntiatum fuisset, quod
scilicet regio eius fuerit ab extraneis devastata, Theudobertum, filium suum,
in illis partibus cum valido exercitu ac magno armorum apparatu direxit.
Qui, interfectu rege, hostibus navali proelio superatis oppraemit omneque
rapinam terrae restituit."

18

THE SONS OF CLOVIS

strong force "cum . . . magno armorum apparatu" — with extensive military equipment. There is no record, however, of the Franks as an ethnic group taking part in any noteworthy naval activity either before or after this event. It should be recalled that when Clovis besieged Paris twenty-five years earlier, he did not have sufficient naval forces to keep the city from being supplied by water. All this suggests that at least a part of Theudebert's *validus exercitus* was not composed of Franks. The abundance of sophisticated military equipment noted by Gregory also implies that there was probably a non-Frankish element in Theudebert's army on this occasion.[2]

The sources provide little information concerning the Merovingian military between the defeat of the Danes in 515 and Theuderic's Thuringian campaign in 531. Shortly after Theudebert's encounter with the Danes, Theuderic aided one of the Thuringian kings in a civil war; in return for this support he had been promised a share in whatever land was conquered. Although territory was taken, Theuderic, much to his dismay, did not receive his share.[3] Some fifteen years later, he felt ready to take not only what he regarded was his, but more. He enlisted the help of his brother Chlotar I and Theudebert, assembled his forces, and moved into Thuringia. The Thuringians, learning of the Franks' approach, dug ditches in the field where they knew a battle would be joined and covered them with sod so that the approaching Frankish horsemen could not see the trap. When the Franks charged across the field to attack the Thuringians, who were waiting for them on the far side, the horses were tripped up by the ditches. This stratagem broke the momentum of the Frankish cavalry charge, but Theuderic's forces managed to recover and finally defeated the Thuringians.[4]

[2] Cf. E. Zöllner, *Geschichte der Franken* (Munich, 1970), p. 153.
[3] Gregory, *Hist.*, III, 4.
[4] *Ibid.*, III, 7: "Theudoricus autem, Chlothacharium fratrem et Theudobertum filium in solatio suo adsumptos, cum exercito abiit. Thoringi vero venientibus Francis dolos praeparant. In campum enim, quo certamen agi debebant, fossas effodiunt, quarum ora operta denso cispete planum adsimilant campum. In his ergo foveis, cum pugnare coepissent, multi Francorum equites conruerunt, et fuit eis valde inpedimentum; sed cognitum hunc dolum, observare coeperunt. Denique cum se Thoringi caedi vehementer

19

Although troops other than Franks probably took part in Theudebert's naval campaign against the Danes, Gregory indicates specifically that only Franks (*Franci*) formed the army which invaded Thuringia, and that the primary striking force, if not indeed the entire force, was mounted. Hermanfrid, the Thuringian king, had fought side by side with Theuderic fifteen years earlier, but his knowledge of the Merovingians' tactics proved to be of no avail. For, even though he had expected the enemy to fight as cavalry and had oriented his defense along those lines, the Franks were still victorious in their mounted attack.

Despite the adeptness of Theuderic's Frankish followers in mounted combat, they seem to have been less than adequate in siege warfare. This weakness was demonstrated in the Auvergne campaign in 532 and the Munderic affair.

While Theuderic was in Thuringia, a rumor spread in Auvergne that he had been killed in battle, and in consequence some Arvernians invited King Childebert to take possession of their district. This attempted change in leadership came to naught, however, when it was learned that Theuderic was, in fact, alive. In the following year, Theuderic planned to avenge himself against the Arvernians for their treachery, but the Franks who looked to him as their king wanted him to join in the attack on Burgundy planned by his brothers Childebert and Chlotar. The Franks threatened to desert him and follow his brothers if he did not attack Burgundy, and it was only after he promised them they would obtain much booty and could keep all they took, even the inhabitants as slaves, that they followed him to Auvergne. Theuderic and his Franks devastated the territory. A raid was made on the Church of St. Julien at Brioude; the fort at Vollore (*Lovolautrum castrum*) was besieged and stormed, but the garrison of *laeti* was taken only by treachery; the fort at Chastel-Marlhac (*Meroliacense castrum*) also withstood a

---

viderent, fugato Hermanefredo rege ipsorum, terga vertunt et ad Onestrudem fluvium usque perveniunt." On the Thuringian campaigns see R. Leibmann, *Der Untergang des thuringischen Königsreichs in den Jahren 531–5* (Meiningen, 1911).

siege. At Chastel-Marlhac part of the garrison became overconfident, and in attempting to sack the enemy camp, it was captured. The defenders had to ransom the captives for a *triens* each.[5] When Theuderic was satisfied that he had taught the Arvernians a lesson, he returned to the north. He granted lands in Auvergne to his kinsman Sigivald, who in turn was to garrison the area with his followers.[6]

It is interesting to note here that the fortifications of Chastel-Marlhac and Vollore, with their garrisons of *laeti*, mark direct continuity with the Roman past, both in the physical structures being defended and in their defenders, who were a *corpus publicum* under the empire and had passed with the fortifications to the Merovingian kings. These *laeti* may also be identified as descendants of Sueve military colonists stationed in that area and listed in the *Notitia Dignitatum*.[7]

Theuderic's stratagems in the Auvergne campaign had proved to be superior to his strategy and made up for his forces' inability to reduce fortified positions by siege. Such also was the case in the Munderic affair. Munderic was a Frank who owned large estates probably in the region of Vitry-le-Brûle near Châlons-sur-Marne; he claimed to be of royal blood and tried to obtain a part of Theuderic's kingdom. He gathered around himself a band of armed men who swore to be his faithful followers. Theuderic attempted to lure him to his court, but failed and therefore ordered a force to be sent against the pretender. Munderic withdrew with his followers behind the walls of Vitry (*Victoriacus castrum*). Theuderic's army laid siege to the fortress, but because they lacked siege engines and even the *magnus aparatus armorum* which Theudebert had employed against the Danes, they could only hurl their spears at the defenders on the walls. After seven days of such futile activity, Theuderic was in-

[5] Gregory, *Hist.*, III, 11; III, 12, 13; Gregory, *Jul.*, ch. 13.
[6] Gregory, *Jul.*, ch. 14: "Tunc Sigivaldus cum rege praepotens cum omni familia sua in Arverna regione ex regis jussu migravit. . . ." See Bernard S. Bachrach, "Charles Martel, Mounted Shock Combat, the Stirrup, and Feudalism," *Studies in Medieval and Renaissance History*, VII (1970), 68–72.
[7] *Notitia Dignitatum, oc.*, LXII, 44: "Praefectus laetorum gentilium Suevorum, Arumbernos Aquitanicae primae."

formed by his commander that it was impossible to take the fortress.[8] Theuderic then sent a group led by Arigisel, one of his personal retainers, to entice Munderic out of Vitry. After taking many oaths of peace and friendship, Arigisel managed to lure Munderic out of the fortress; once outside he and his followers were cut down in a bloody hand-to-hand combat.[9] Theuderic's appointment of Arigisel to lead this expedition indicates that the king had a structure of command within his military organization. Arigisel's mission represents the second time, so far as can be ascertained, that Theuderic delegated command to someone other than his son. The first to have been so distinguished was Sigivald, who had been given a command in Auvergne.

In contrast to the weakness of Theuderic's Frankish followers in siege warfare, the forces from the south of Gaul led by his son Theudebert and his brothers Chlotar and Childebert were considerably more effective in siege operations. This may be attributed to the fact that they recruited their troops from the more Romanized parts of Gaul. Theudebert and his army conquered the Gothic fortress city of Béziers in southern Gaul, and then seized and sacked the fortress of Dio to the north of Béziers. Cabriers capitulated to Theudebert after learning the fate of Dio.[10]

The most important result of successful siege warfare was the conquest of the Burgundian kingdom by Chlotar and Childebert in 534. By besieging Autun, the headquarters of Godomar, the Burgundian king, they were able to take the city, causing the monarch to flee. The ultimate consequence was the subjugation of the entire Burgundian realm to Merovingian control.[11] With this conquest, the Merovingian kings added the lands, wealth, population, and military resources of the Burgundian kingdom to their own holdings. A more important effect of this victory, however, was the further penetration of Roman influences into

[8] Gregory, *Hist.*, III, 14.
[9] *Ibid.*; Fred., III, 36.
[10] Gregory, *Hist.*, III, 21. See Longnon, *Géographie*, pp. 611–612.
[11] Gregory, *Hist.*, III, 11.

the Merovingian military and political structure. The Burgundian military had for some time seen the syncretism of barbarian and Roman institutions. From the second half of the fifth century, Gallo-Romans served in the Burgundian army. In addition there was at least one noteworthy unit in the Burgundian military which was composed completely of Gallo-Romans.[12]

The important men of the kingdom, Gallo-Roman and Burgundian magnates alike, had for a long time supported private bands of armed retainers. Sidonius Apollinaris, whose writings provide a great deal of information on late Roman society in the Burgundian kingdom, praises his son-in-law Ecdicius for using his private army against the Visigoths as a public service. On another occasion, however, Sidonius complains bitterly to his friend Thaumastus about certain important men whose access to the Burgundian king endangers the favored position usually enjoyed by the Gallo-Roman senatorials. Among Sidonius's criticisms of these men is their lack of noblesse oblige. In this vein he contends that they not only failed to provide their military retainers with the stipend which was due them, but also deprived their bodyguards of the sustenance they required. He writes: "hi sunt, qui invident . . . stipendia paludatis . . . praetorianis sportulas. . . ."[13] Of course, Sidonius is exaggerating the degeneracy of his enemies. These men surely would be the last to weaken their positions by neglecting their military retainers and bodyguards. The *sportulae* which were due the bodyguards (whom Sidonius pedantically calls *praetoriani*) may be compared to the *buccellata* from which the *buccellarii* got their name. A more prosaic writer might have used a term like *sportularii* to describe these guards because they were provided with *sportulae*. The military retainers who received the *stipen-*

---

[12] L. Musset, *Les invasiones*, 2nd ed. (Paris, 1969), pp. 114ff, 247ff; E. A. Thompson, "The Barbarian Kingdoms in Gaul and Spain," *Nottingham Mediaeval Studies*, VII (1963), 9. *L.B.* (*prim. cons't.*), no. 5; *Lex Rom. Burg.*, XLV, 3; and V. *Eptadii*, ch. 12, for the Roman force in the Burgundian army. Procopius, *H.W.*, V, xiii, 3, for the use of Burgundian military forces by the Merovingian kings.

[13] Sidonius Apollinaris, *ep.* V, 7, 3. On Sidonius see C. E. Stevens, *Sidonius Apollinaris and His Age* (Oxford, 1933).

dia paludatis were probably former Roman soldiers who continued to wear at least part of their uniforms — namely, the cloak (*paludamentum*). Procopius, writing almost a century later, noted that even in his day the descendants of erstwhile Roman soldiers in Gaul still wore their uniforms. During the later Roman empire imperial military officers often became local magnates and used their troops in essentially private capacities. These magnates were neither senatorials nor barbarians; nevertheless they had considerable influence and power.[14]

The magnates of the Burgundians drew their armed followers from diverse sources. Slaves were used as well as non-Burgundian barbarians. Sigismir, a Burgundian prince, supported a large armed force which included Franks among his horsemen. Whereas some of Sigismir's *socii* were Franks of no noteworthy rank, others of his *socii* were *reguli* or kinglets with *socii* of their own. This points to a command structure among the armed retainers of at least one important magnate.[15]

The Burgundian monarchs, in addition to their personal armed followers, used mercenaries to garrison the forts and walled cities of their kingdoms. Such a garrison served at Vienne in 502 during Clovis's invasion of the Burgundian kingdom. A part of this garrison included Frankish mercenaries while another, composed of archers, may have been what remained of an imperial regiment.[16] Among the more important fortified places in the Burgundian kingdom were Lyons, Avenches, Geneva, Grenoble, Vienne, Langres, Dijon, Autun, and Besançon, which also had two regiments of Roman cavalry (*milites*). *Milites* as well as *laeti* were stationed at Langres, and there were also probably *laeti* at Autun. In addition to the *laeti* and *milites*, who as descendants of military colonists and regular soldiers garrisoned the fortified places of the Burgundian lands, there were a number of Burgundian magnates who received land from the king

---

[14] See MacMullen, *Soldier and Citizen*, ch. 6, and ch. I, n. 43, above.

[15] Sidonius Apollinaris, *ep.* IV, 20, 1, 2, 3; Gregory, *Hist.*, III, 5; *L.B.*, II, 3, 4; V, 7; X, 1.

[16] Gregory, *Hist.*, II, 32, 33; *V. Epiphanii*, 171; Procopius, *H.W.*, V, xii, 29; xiii, 3.

in return for their services as garrison commanders similar to *centenarii*.[17]

If the simple Burgundian freeman, because of his legal status, had ever owed military service in a general levy of some kind, such an obligation probably had disappeared before the end of the fifth century when the Burgundian laws were written down, for they make no mention of this military responsibility. It may be hypothesized that all able-bodied men in the kingdom could be called upon to take up whatever arms might be at hand for the needs of local defense, and it seems equally likely that when a campaign in which plunder might be obtained was to be undertaken, at least some hardy souls would heed the call of adventure, though they were not required to do so by either law or custom. By and large, however, the backbone of the Burgundian military, as it passed under Merovingian domination in 534, was not made up of these temporary soldiers, but of *laeti* and *milites*, erstwhile imperial fighting men, and the armed followings of the royal family and magnates.

After the conquest of the Burgundian kingdom, the Merovingian monarchs might have concentrated their efforts on the invasion of new lands. Instead, they insisted upon fighting among themselves. In the same year that the Burgundians yielded to the military might of the Merovingians, Gregory reports, Theudebert and Childebert agreed to attack Chlotar. Fortuitously for the new allies, they learned that Chlotar was traveling southward through his kingdom; on his journey he had to cross Childebert's lands. The allies caught Chlotar and his small following off guard on the south bank of the Seine, just across from the village of Caudebec, about twenty-two miles westnorthwest of Rouen.[18] Realizing that he could neither escape nor defeat his enemies' superior force in an open battle, Chlotar retreated into the Forest of Arelaunum where he ordered trees

[17] Butler, "Late Roman Town Walls in Gaul," pp. 48–50; Gregory, *V.P.*, VII, 4; "Cumque milites cum aequitibus praecedentes, cum post terga traherent vinctum, ad locum ubi confessoris artus quieverant pervenerunt." *Notitia Dignitatum, oc.*, XLII, 69, 70; XXXVI, 5. Grenier, *Manuel d' archéologie*, V, 400, n. 2. *L.B.*, I, especially no. 4.

[18] Gregory, *Hist.*, III, 28; *L.H.F.*, ch. 25. Longnon, *Géographie*, p. 137.

to be cut down and barricades to be built; this made his position less accessible and provided him with additional cover. Childebert and Theudebert surrounded Chlotar's position, pitched camp, tethered their mounts, which were not of much use in the heavy forest (explaining in part Chlotar's defensive tactics), and prepared to attack Chlotar's stronghold in the morning. However, in the morning a hailstorm accompanied by lightning and thunder struck the attackers' camp. blowing away their tents, and scattering their mounts. The disaster demoralized them to the extent that they broke off the engagement and made peace.[19] Small campaigns like this one seem to interest Gregory because he is able to credit St. Martin with bringing the storm against the brothers and saving Chlotar. On the other hand, more important engagements — the invasions of Burgundy in 523, 524, and 534, Childebert's victory over Amalaric, the Visigothic king, in 531, and the lengthy though unsuccessful siege of Saragossa undertaken by Chlotar and Childebert in 542 — receive comparatively little notice and are described with scarcely any military details.[20]

The conquest of Burgundy in 534 had brought the Merovingian monarchs into closer contact with Italy. During the reigns of the Austrasian monarchs Theudebert and his son Theudebald, campaigns were undertaken in Italy in 539 and 554; these received little attention in the Merovingian sources, but were much publicized by the Byzantine authors Procopius and Agathias. In 539, Theudebert, aware that the Ostrogothic and Byzantine armies were hard pressed in their war, decided to lead an expedition into Italy. Both the Gothic and imperial commanders believed Theudebert to be on their side and no effort was made to stop the advance of his army, extravagantly estimated at 100,000 fighting men by Procopius. Both the Goths and the Byzantines welcomed Theudebert's army and were cut down in turn. After these intial successes and the acquisition of

<hr/>

[19] Gregory, *Hist.*, III, 28.

[20] *Ibid.*, III, 6, 10, 11, 29; Isid., *Hist. Goth.*, DLVIII; *Chron. Caesaraug.*, s.a., 541; Jordanes, *Get.*, lviii, 302. Thompson, *The Goths in Spain*, pp. 12–15.

a considerable amount of booty, lack of supplies and disease weakened the invaders and they retreated north into Gaul. The lack of an organized system of supply defeated Theudebert's army where the armies of the empire and the Ostrogoths could not.[21]

The campaign of 554 differed in many ways from that of 539. Theudebald was a weak and sickly monarch, nothing like his father. Where the latter himself had led the earlier Italian invasion, Theudebald entrusted the campaign of 554 to a pair of Alaman magnates, Buccelin and Leutharis, who Agathias exaggeratedly states led a force of some 75,000 Franks and Alamans into Italy. After taking Parma and Pavia, the invaders moved toward Rome, where they divided into two groups. One, under the command of Buccelin, bypassed Rome and went south to Messina; the other force, under Leutharis, went through Apulia and Calabria to Hydruntum. Both chiefs are said to have collected a huge amount of booty, some of which was sent back to Gaul. On the return to Gaul, Leutharis's troops, forced to fight on foot, suffered severe setbacks from the Roman garrison at Pisaurum and lost much booty. Continuing north, Leutharis's forces camped at Ceneta where a plague broke out killing many of the invaders, including their commander. Buccelin returned to the north by way of Campania. While camping at Casilinum, he engaged in a battle against an imperial army under Narses. Buccelin's forces, fighting on foot, were trapped in a crossfire by Narses's mounted archers and were destroyed.[22]

In this campaign there was another noteworthy battle in which Narses destroyed a small group of invaders. This band, composed about equally of infantry and cavalry, deployed in a phalanx in a forest and faced Narses's cavalry. Narses ordered a charge, and his horsemen, after some contact, feigned a disorderly retreat. The Merovingian troops broke ranks and pur-

---

[21] Procopius, *H.W.*, VI, xxv, 11; Gregory, *Hist.*, III, 32. See Bernard S. Bachrach, "Procopius, Agathias, and the Frankish Military," *Speculum*, XLV (1970), 435–441, and the appendix below, pp. 131–138.

[22] Agathias, *Hist.*, I, 6; II, 2, 8, 9; Gregory, *Hist.*, III, 32. J. B. Bury, *History of the Later Roman Empire* (New York, 1958), II, 277ff; Bachrach, "Procopius, Agathias," pp. 435–441, and the appendix below, pp. 131–138.

sued them, but the Byzantines turned their horses and slaughtered the scattered infantry, winning the day. The Merovingian horsemen, however, fled to safety.[23]

Apart from these invasions of Italy, only two other campaigns of this period — Chlotar's campaigns against the Saxons and against his rebellious son, Chramn — are described in the sources in sufficient detail to be useful. After Theudebald's death in 555, Chlotar had inherited his lands. While making a progress through his newly acquired Austrasian kingdom in the following year, Chlotar learned that the Saxons had rebelled again and so he moved against them. When he approached their borders, the Saxons sent envoys seeking peace. Chlotar was willing to reestablish peace, but the Austrasian Franks in his entourage would not hear of it and attacked Chlotar. Gregory suggests that they would perhaps even have killed him had he refused to fight. The Franks' bellicosity, however, seems to have been more manifest in counsel than on the battlefield, for when they met the Saxons on the field they were decisively defeated.[24]

Chlotar's most pressing problem, however, seems to have been his son Chramn, who led a warband of mounted followers and was served by two officers, Scapthar and Imnachar, whom Gregory describes as the leaders of his bodyguard. Chramn made his headquarters at Clermont, where he had driven out the Count Firminus. He harassed the area by seizing women and terrorizing Bishop Cautinus, who kept a saddled horse at his side to escape being ridden down by Chramn's followers.[25] Chramn's activities led him to abandon Auvergne and to move to Poitiers, where he made his new headquarters. Shortly thereafter, he allied with his uncle Childebert with the aim of going against his father in force. Chlotar finally acted and sent his sons Charibert and Guntram against Chramn, who was at that time encamped at Black Mountain in the Limousin. Negotiations proved futile and the opponents prepared for the battle with "magno

[23] Agathias, *Hist.*, I, 21. Bernard S. Bachrach, "The Feigned Retreat at Hastings," pp. 265–266.

[24] Gregory, *Hist.*, IV, 14.

[25] *Ibid.*, IV, 13.

armorum apparatu," but when both forces were about to engage, a storm broke with thunder and lightning and each side returned to camp. Chramn then forged a message to his brothers saying that their father had been killed in battle against the Saxons. Charibert and Guntram mounted and left with all speed, returning to Burgundy. Chramn followed with his force and moved against Châlons-sur-Marne, which he took after a siege. He continued on to Dijon, but did not enter, and then proceeded to Paris where he met with Childebert.[26]

Chramn continued his operations against his father by moving against the governor of Theiphalia, while Childebert seized Rheims. Shortly thereafter, however, Childebert died and Chramn, unable to come to terms with his father, fled to Brittany where he found an ally in Count Chanao. Chlotar moved his forces into Brittany and a battle was fought against Chramn and the count. Chanao fled the field soon after the battle had begun, and Chramn, as he retreated to the ships which he had prepared for his escape in case of disaster, was captured and killed.[27]

Chramn's activity in 556 illustrates not only the mobility of his forces, but their ability to take a fortified position. This may have been due to the military equipment which his troops, like those of his brothers, carried with them. All three princes made their home in, and presumably drew their forces from, the more Romanized parts of Gaul — suggesting the influence of imperial military traditions on Merovingian warfare.

Chramn's activities and those of the pretender, Munderic, are described in considerable detail by Gregory, who in doing so indicates the role which personal armed followings played in the struggle for power. These personal armed followings differed from each other just as did the men who led them. Chramn, a prince of royal blood, controlled a comparatively large, well-organized personal following, commanded by officers, mounted, and armed with an abundance of sophisticated military equipment. This force constituted nothing less than a private army.

[26] Ibid., IV, 16, 17.
[27] Ibid., IV, 18, 20.

Munderic's group, on the other hand, was not organized under a command structure, but was a more amorphous unit of sworn men who nevertheless fought with epic spirit. Arigisel also had armed supporters (although surely not of the magnitude of Chramn's band), as did another of Theuderic's retainers, a barbarian (Frank?) who directed certain royal estates for the breeding and raising of horses near Trèves. Sigivald, whom Theuderic provided with land in return for his garrisoning the Auvergne after the revolt of 531, had an armed following with which he plundered the area he was required to protect. Gallo-Romans, as noted above, also had personal armed retainers, which they employed to gain various ends. For example, Syagrius, a member of the famous noble family which flourished in Gaul during the late empire and early Middle Ages, used his retainers to help him liquidate his enemy Syrivald, the son of Sigivald. Men like Sigivald, Syagrius, Munderic, and Bishop Cautinus were landowners, but possessed neither the stature nor the prestige of one such as Chramn. Munderic's claim to royal blood, Sigivald's kinship with Theuderic, and Syagrius's family connections did augment their importance, but never did they attain an equal footing with a prince. These men shared a relatively similar position in society not only because they all controlled armed forces, but also because of their comparable relations with the humble peasant, small landholder, and economic dependent whom they exploited and harassed.[28]

Loyalty and support from these magnates (if such a term may be used to describe these landholders with armed followings) were vital to any monarch who hoped to rule successfully. The tumult caused by Munderic's attempted usurpation and by Chramn's activities underscores this point well. Equally illuminating is an event which took place shortly after Theuderic's death in 533. When Theudebert tried to succeed his father, he found that his uncles Chlotar and Childebert were planning to bar his way. Theudebert, however, gained the support of his *leudes* with gifts, and with their aid was able to ascend the

[28] *Ibid.*, III, 15, 16, 35; IV, 12. Bachrach, "Charles Martel," pp. 71–72.

THE SONS OF CLOVIS

throne.[29] The significance of the *leudes* has already been suggested in the description of Clovis's victory over Ragnachar in 509. When Clovis went against Ragnachar, he bribed his enemy's *leudes* and thus deprived him of his military followers.[30] Theudebert, unlike Ragnachar, was able to gain the support of his *leudes,* and thus prevailed against his uncles. Another example of the significance of such followers to a ruler concerns Chlotar's son Chilperic, who when his father died in 561, used a part of the royal treasure which fell into his hands to ensure the support of those men whom he thought would be of value to his cause. To strengthen his position still further, Chilperic permitted his supporters (*fideles*) to plunder and seize estates within his kingdom, thus buying their loyalty with wealth that was not his to give.[31] It is probable that the kind of men whose support ensured Theudebert's succession and whose loyalty Chilperic tried to purchase were of that group who controlled bands of armed followers — men very much like Sigivald and Syagrius, who when serving in the royal interest could help to keep a king in power, but when alienated could weaken his position greatly.

Among the Austrasian Franks in particular, important men of this type asserted their influence in military matters most conspicuously. When Theuderic wanted to invade Thuringia in 531, he had to go to great lengths to convince these men and their retainers to follow him. Ultimately they consented and distinguished themselves in a cavalry charge on the Thuringian plains. When, in the following year, Theuderic wanted to punish the Arvernians for their revolt, these Franks with their armed supporters threatened to desert him and to follow his brothers

[29] Gregory, *Hist.,* III, 23: "Cumque abissit, Theodoricus non post multos dies obiit vicinsimo tertio regni sui anno. Consurgentes autem Childeberthus et Chlothacharius contra Theudobertum, regnum eius auferre voluerunt, sed ille muneribus placatis a leodibus suis defensatus est et in regnum stabilitus."

[30] *Ibid.,* II, 42.

[31] *Ibid.,* IV, 22: "Chilpericus vero post patris funera thesaurus, qui in villa Brannacum erant congregati, accepit et ad Francos utiliores petiit ipsusque muneribus mollitus sibi subdidit." VII, 7: "Guntchramnus vero rex omnia quae fidelis regis Chilperici non recte diversis abstulerant . . . restituit. . . ." Bachrach, "Charles Martel," pp. 71–72.

who were planning an invasion of Burgundy. As has already been mentioned, it was not until Theuderic promised them an abundance of booty in gold, silver, slaves, and raiment, as well as the right to keep everything they seized including the inhabitants, that they followed him into Auvergne. The enormous power of the Austrasian magnates was also exemplified when Chlotar's Frankish followers threatened to kill him if he accepted a treaty with the Saxons who were harassing his border in 556.[32]

Yet another aspect of the personal armed following deserves notice, that relating to the role of the king's guards. While on campaign in Thuringia in 531, Chlotar's life was saved by the armed men (*armati*) who surrounded his person. Certain guards (*pueri*) who normally served Queen Clotild, Clovis's widow, were assigned by her to protect her nephews, the sons of the deceased Chlodomer. Arigisel may be considered part of Theuderic's guard.[33] The identification of such guards with the *antrustiones* or members of the royal *trust* suggests a force of considerable size and scope. Men of the royal trust not only served at the king's side, but were also stationed in *centenae* established throughout Gaul. These *centenae* were used by the Merovingian kings for both colonizing and military purposes. Among the inhabitants of the *centenae* were the *antrustiones* who probably performed military and paramilitary services required of them under the command of the *centenarius,* a royal official of imperial origin. Since the *antrustiones* were composed of *laeti* and Romans as well as Franks and other barbarians, it is likely that the military functions of these settlements had some connection with the military colonies of *laeti* and other garrisons which had been established earlier by the empire.[34]

---

[32] Gregory, *Hist.*, IV, 14.

[33] *Ibid.*, III, 7, 18.

[34] For a convincing definition of the *centena* see Wallace-Hadrill, *Long-Haired Kings,* p. 193, n. 1, and cf. H. Dannenbauer, "Die Freien im karolingische Heer," *Aus Verfassungs- und Landesgeschichte: Festschrift für T. Mayer* (Lindau, 1954), I, 49–64. MGH Cap., I, 3, 16: "Pro tenere pacis iubemus, ut in truste electi centenarii ponantur, per quorum fidem adque sollicitudinem pax praedicta observetur. Et quia propiciante Domino inter nos germanitatis caritas, indisruptum vinculum, custoditur, centenarii inter communes provincias licentiam habeant latrones persequere vel vestigia

THE SONS OF CLOVIS

Any effort to estimate the size of the Merovingian military organization founders upon the predilection of chroniclers for exaggeration. In only one text — a copy of a letter from Theudebert to Justinian in which he apologizes for not having sent the emperor the 3000 troops he had promised him during the preceding year — is a reliable figure probably given.[35] This epistle implies that Theudebert had at his disposal during the late 530s a force large enough so that he could spare 3000 men and still maintain his own position. In any event, it seems unlikely that Theudebert believed he could count on the followers of the ill-disciplined Austrasian magnates whose caprice and greed made them unreliable in the extreme. It might be suggested, however, that Theudebert had considered sending a unit from the Burgundian kingdom, which was reliable and well disciplined.[36]

This picture of the Merovingian military under Clovis's sons is necessarily incomplete, since the answers to many questions simply cannot be found. Nevertheless, it can be discerned that the *milites* who garrisoned fortifications, the *laeti* who protected fortresses and served as *antrustiones* in *centenae*, the personal armed followings of the magnates, as well as other remnants of the later Roman military establishment were militarily significant.[37] The Taifal *laeti* living in the area around Poitiers may have been used as garrison troops, though the sources are mute on the point; in any event, Theiphalia was organized under a *dux*.[38] This use of erstwhile imperial military formations

---

adsignata minare et in truste quod defecerit, sicut dictum est causa remaneat, ita ut continuo capitale ei qui perdiderit reformare festinet, tamen ut latronem perquirat. Quem si in truste pervenerit, medietatem sibi vindicet, vel dilatura si fuerit, de facultate latronis ei qui damnum pertulit sarciatur." See also *Lex Sal.*, XLII, 1–4.

[35] *MGH, ep.*, III, 19. F. Lot, *L'Art militaire et les armées au moyen âge en Europe et dans le proche orient* (Paris, 1946), I, 78–79, discusses this letter in some detail.

[36] Procopius, *H.W.*, VI, xii, 38, suggests that Theudebert also agreed to send aid to the Ostrogoths and in fact sent 10,000 Burgundians. Although the number is most probably exaggerated, it can be assumed that Theudebert had it within his power to use Burgundian troops.

[37] *Notitia Dignitatum, oc.*, LXII, 44.

[38] Gregory, *Hist.*, IV, 18, and ch. 1, n. 30, above.

33

was supplemented by the use of Roman fortifications throughout Gaul.

The utilization of past imperial forms of organization as well as the descendants of Roman personnel is illustrated by the situation at Langres. This fortified city, which served as a military base under the empire, continued its original function under Clovis and his sons. The Sarmatian *laeti* who were settled there during the later Roman empire gave their names to towns and villages in the area — for example, Salmaise (Latin, *Sarmatia*). One of the suburbs (modern Lassois) was known throughout the Middle Ages as the *laeti* quarter, *Laticensus*. This section of the city was under the direct control of an official of the king's household. During the reign of Theudebert, a Gallo-Roman of distinguished parentage named Valentinus held the position. In addition to the *laeti* serving at Langres there were also mounted *milites*, according to Gregory.[39] This notice of *milites* at Langres is only one of several such references in the sources to *milites*, which at times are depicted as serving under *tribuni*.[40] Other Roman influences are suggested by Gregory's cryptic passages concerning military equipment which was used to great advantage by both Theudebert and Chramn. And it can perhaps be ascertained that Roman elements lingered to affect Merovingian naval organization and provided the men and ships which defeated the Danes in 515. In the general area of this encounter, there had been an

---

[39] *V. Valent.*, ch. I: "Beatus Valentinus in Laticensi suburbano Lingonensium oriundus fuit: parentibus nobilibus ortus, trahens ex paterni generis sanguine originem a Romanis. Cujus pueritia futuram virtutem jam tunc praeclara indole depingebat. Peridem tempus Theodebertus Rex una cum fratribus Francorum regnum potenter regebat: sub quo Palatinam militiam praedictus vir in adolescentia pro dignitate parentum administravit. . . ." Gregory, *V.P.*, VII, 4: "Cumque milites cum aequitibus. . . ." Longnon, *Géographie*, p. 101, n. 4, identifies Lassois and defends the reliability of the *V. Valent.* as a historical source. See also Edgard Boutaric, *Institutions militaires de la France avant les armées permanentes* (Paris, 1863), p. 66. *Notitia Dignitatum, oc.*, XLII, 69: "Praefectus Sarmatarum gentilium, Lingonas." On place names see L. Berthoud and L. Matruchot, *Étude Historique et étymologique des noms de lieux habités du département de la Côte-D'Or* (Semur, 1901), I, 2.

[40] *V. Genov.*, ch. 36, and ch. I, n. 5, above.

imperial naval base during the fifth century.[41] Whether Roman or not, the fleet which served Theudebert in northern Gaul and the ships prepared by Chramn were not of Frankish origin. The Frankish role in Merovingian military organization during the reign of Clovis's sons, although overestimated in most scholarly accounts, should nevertheless not be underestimated, even if by such underestimation a valuable corrective to the popular view might be supplied. Frankish units seem to have had an important function in Austrasia, the least Romanized region of Gaul. Large numbers of Franks played a significant part in the Italian campaign of 539, and Franks as well as Alamans served in large numbers in the Italian venture of 554. The descriptions of the Franks who participated in these transalpine operations indicate that they were even less Romanized than were the Franks of Austrasia. Many of the Franks used in the Italian campaigns were probably recruited by the Austrasian monarchs from beyond the Rhine. In doing this Theudebert and Theudebald seem to have initiated a policy which was developed during the next generation by Sigibert, their successor in Austrasia.[42]

The diverse development of the Merovingian military organization, which had been manifest under Clovis, continued along the same lines under his sons. The heterogeneous ethnic composition of the military forces, including Franks, Alamans, Gallo-Romans, descendants of imperial military personnel, Alans, Saxons, and Taifals, was expanded by Clovis's sons with the inclusion of the Burgundians and their military establishment. The complexity of this organization as it passed into the hands of Clovis's grandsons defies simple characterization, although its Roman elements are worth emphasizing in light of previous scholarly neglect.

[41] *Notitia Dignitatum, oc.*, XXXVIII, 8: "Praefectus classis Sambricae, in loco Quartensi sivi Hornensi." Grenier, *Manuel d'archéologie*, V, 390ff.
[42] Gregory, *Hist.*, IV, 49, 50. Cf. A. Cameron, "Agathias on the Early Merovingians," *Annali della Scuola Normale Superiore di Pisa*, XXXVII (1968), 129ff, 136–140. Appendix, n. 7, for the trans-Rhenish origin and the primitive nature of the Merovingian armies in the Italian campaigns.

CHAPTER III

Clovis's Grandsons: 561–593

W HEN Chlotar died in 561, Merovingian military activity continued under the leadership of his sons Chilperic, Sigibert, Guntram, and Charibert, each of whom received a share of Chlotar's kingdom. Although the period of their reigns was plagued by internal fighting, the military organization begun by Clovis increased in power and complexity with the introduction of a new fighting force — the local levy.

561–575

The year after Chlotar's death, when Sigibert was called upon to defend his eastern border against the Avars, Chilperic invaded the western part of his kingdom, taking possession of Rheims, Soissons, and several other cities which Gregory does not name. Upon successfully driving out the Avars, Sigibert moved west and retook these cities; at Soissons he captured Chilperic's son Theudebert, who had been left there to command a garrison. This incident touched off the first spark that eventually flared up into the *bella civilia* which were to characterize the reigns of Clovis's grandsons.[1]

Approximately four years after Sigibert defeated the Avars, these barbarians once again attacked the Merovingian kingdom. Sigibert went to meet them in battle, but in this encounter he

---

[1] Gregory, *Hist.*, IV, 23. Wallace-Hadrill, *Long-Haired Kings*, p. 195.

was not as fortunate as he had been in 562. According to Gregory, his forces became so frightened by fantastic shapes which the Avars made to appear before them through the use of magic that they fled the field. Sigibert, abandoned by his army, arranged a treaty with the Avar leader after giving him rich presents. Because of this treaty, the Avars made no more attacks against Sigibert's lands during his lifetime.[2] Gregory, desiring to protect the reputation of Sigibert, to whom he was partial, contends that the treaty may be counted to his credit. It is probable that Sigibert's treaty called for a yearly tribute to be paid to the Avars, and that his forces were not capable of thwarting a concerted Avar effort. In short, Sigibert bought peace when he had little or no hope of winning it.

In 568 Sigibert expanded the *bella civilia* by attacking his brother Guntram. According to a provision in Chlotar's will, the city of Arles was divided between Sigibert and Guntram, and now the former wanted all of it. He ordered Count Firminus of Clermont to lead the Arvernians against Arles and to take control of the city. (This order is the earliest extant reference in the Merovingian sources to a local levy.) Sigibert also commanded a certain Audovar to lead a force from the other direction which seems to have been raised or stationed in Provence (perhaps near Aix) against Arles. Both leaders entered Arles unopposed, and they proceeded to take oaths of fealty to Sigibert from the inhabitants. As soon as Guntram learned that Sigibert's forces had seized Arles, he sent the partician Celsus with a force to retake the city. On the way to Arles, Celsus took Avignon without a battle. Arriving at Arles, he surrounded the city and commenced his attack. Sigibert's officers were convinced that they could not defend the city against a siege so they sallied forth in the hope of routing Celsus's forces. Sigibert's troops, however, were soundly defeated, and when they tried to reenter Arles, the gates were locked and the inhabitants hurled stones on them from the walls. With all hope of victory lost, they abandoned their mounts and tried

[2] Gregory, *Hist.*, IV, 29.

to swim across the Rhone. A large number of Arvernians were lost, including many noteworthy citizens. Firminus and Audovar were captured but were later released unharmed.[3]

The year before this animosity between Sigibert and Guntram developed, their brother Charibert had died, and his kingdom was divided among his brothers. Although little is known of Charibert's military campaigns, Gregory does discuss in some detail one of his paramilitary operations because it involved the alleged intervention of St. Martin. Greogry relates that Charibert, upon learning that the Church of Tours had illegally come into possession of a royal estate where horses were bred, dispatched a group of mounted and armed *pueri* from his court to take over the estate and to protect the wranglers and grooms he needed there. Charibert's adventure proved unsuccessful, however, because, according to Gregory, St. Martin routed his men.[4]

With the division of Charibert's kingdom, Sigibert obtained cities in both Neustria and Aquitaine — cities Chilperic coveted. Probably in 569 Chilperic took Tours, which had been part of Sigibert's share, and left the city under the command of his son Chlodovech. In Poitiers he induced important men like Basilius and Sighar to join his cause; they either gave Chilperic their support with armed forces of their own or perhaps they collaborated with royal followers *(pueri regis)*.[5] Even though Sigibert and Guntram had contested the control of Arles, they allied in the following year to stop Chilperic's attacks. This was accomplished with the help of Mummolus, who at the death of Amantus, Celsus's successor, had become patrician. In 570

---

[3] *Ibid.*, IV, 30: "Sigyberthus vero rex Arelatensim urbem capere cupiens, Arvernus commovere praecipit. Erat enim tunc Firminus comes urbis illius, qui cum ipsis in capite abiit. Sed et de alia parte Audovarius cum exercitu advenit." Longnon, *Géographie*, p. 147, for Aix belonging to Sigibert. The words "alia parte" would seem to point to this part of Gaul as contrasted to Clermont.

[4] Gregory, *Virt. S. Mart.*, I, 29. It is curious that Charibert was buried at Blavia castellum, one of the Roman fortifications in the Aquitanian part of the *Tractus Armoricani*. The town was of military importance only. See *L.H.F.*, ch. 31.

[5] Gregory, *Hist.*, IV, 45.

Mummolus was able to move west, driving Chlodovech from Tours and suppressing opposition at Poitiers. As Firminus and Audovar had done in Provence, Mummolus exacted oaths of fealty to Sigibert from the people of Tours and Poitiers.[6]

In the years immediately following this episode, the Merovingian kings undertook two extended series of campaigns. Guntram's forces, led by Mummolus, fought four campaigns in the course of as many years. In 571, hearing that the Lombards had entered Gaul and had advanced to the Plan de Fazi near Embrun, he assembled his forces and trapped the Lombards in the forests by blocking the roads with trees. Once he had nullified the effectiveness of the Lombard horsemen in this way, he attacked them in the woods and cut them to pieces. Those who survived and could not escape were taken prisoner and sent to various strongholds in the Burgundian kingdom where they were kept under guard.[7]

A year after this massacre, a large band of Saxons who had entered Italy in 569 as Lombard allies raided Guntram's lands and encamped at the villa of Stablo in the territory of Riez. When Mummolus learned of their invasion, he moved against them and was able to kill large numbers because they had divided into small groups in order to plunder the countryside. This slaughter continued until nightfall when under cover of the ensuing darkness the remaining Saxons slipped back into their camp. By morning they had regrouped at Stablo and faced Mummolus's forces. A showdown was averted, however, when a peace treaty was arranged. This treaty allowed the Saxons and their families to settle in Sigibert's kingdom. The warriors therefore returned to Italy for their women and children. They reentered Gaul in 573 in two groups, one proceeding through Nice and the other through Embrun. They regrouped at Avignon where they plundered the crops. However, when they prepared to cross the Rhone and enter Sigibert's

[6] *Ibid.*, IV, 42.
[7] *Ibid.*

39

kingdom, Mummolus barred their way and forced them to pay for what they had stolen and destroyed.[8]

In 574 Gaul was invaded once again, this time by a Lombard force under the command of Dukes Amo, Zaban, and Rodan. At Embrun the Lombards deployed into three groups, with Amo leading one group south through Gap and on towards Avignon, camping at Mummolus's villa at Macho. Amo does not seem to have taken Avignon, but he subdued Arles and raided as far as Marseilles. At Aix he collected a tribute of twenty-two pounds of silver and withdrew. Zaban also went south through Gap, but then turned north through Die and on to Valence, which he besieged. Rodan traveled north and west from Embrun and camped near Grenoble to which he laid siege. When Mummolus learned of the Lombard invasion, he immediately moved to attack Rodan at Grenoble. After crossing the Isère, Mummolus's troops engaged the Lombards and defeated them handily. Rodan and his remaining followers fled south to Valence through the mountains and forests of the Dauphiné. Mummolus did not pursue them but, taking advantage of his interior lines of transportation, rode east along the Roman road from Grenoble to Embrun in order to cut off the Lombards' line of retreat into Italy. Along the way Mummolus seems to have gathered a multitude of men from the countryside; with his forces thus enlarged, he awaited the appearance of Rodan and Zaban. As Mummolus had expected, the Lombards reached Embrun and there he dealt them a crushing defeat; only a small number managed to escape and return to Italy. Amo, who had remained in the south and probably spent much of his time in Sigibert's lands of Provence, escaped Guntram's patrician, but was trapped in the Alps by the snows and almost perished.[9]

Gregory's accounts of Mummolus's activity against the Lombards and Celsus's successes at Avignon and Arles offer useful insights into the command structure and military operations of the Merovingian-ruled Burgundian kingdom at this point in his-

[8] *Ibid.*
[9] *Ibid.*, IV, 44. On the roads see Grenier, *Manuel d'archéologie*, VI, fig. 48 and pl. 1.

tory, as well as further evidence of Roman influence on these early medieval institutions. Both Mummolus and Celsus had at their command a standing force capable of rapidly moving into action, rather than a group of warriors which had to be raised (*collectus* or *congregatus*). Gregory, after learning that the Lombards had reached Embrun, claimed that in Mummolus's first campaign he "exercitus movit, et cum Burgundionibus illus proficiscetur." Of the battle against the Saxons, he writes: "Quod cum Mummolus conperisset, exercitum movet," and of the last Lombard campaign: "Qui Mummolo perlata fuissent, exercitum movit." The same conclusion can be drawn from the actions of Celsus's troops when Guntram ordered them to retake Arles as soon as he learned that the city had fallen to Sigibert ("Quod cum Gunthramnus rex conperisset, Celsum patricium cum exercitu illuc dirigit").[10]

The military descriptions offered by Gregory also suggest that Celsus's and Mummolus's forces as well as their structure of command may have been of Roman origin. The rank of patrician held by these commanders seems to have been the title given to the military leaders of the old Burgundian army (many of whom, like Celsus and Mummolus, were Gallo-Romans).[11] As already noted, the Burgundian monarchs had integrated Roman *milites* stationed in their realms into the Burgundian military. And these same *milites* and their descendants may well have formed a standing army (like that of Celsus and of Mummolus) which functioned in the Burgundian kingdom under Merovingian domination and was capable of rapid military response.

Shortly after the Lombard invasion of 571, Guntram and Sigibert were again at odds. Chilperic, aware that his brothers' alliance was in jeopardy and that, even if the rift were healed, a significant part of Guntram's forces would still be involved against the Lombards, moved once more against Sigibert. Chilperic's son Chlodovech established himself at Bordeaux, but not

[10] Gregory, *Hist.*, IV, 30, 42, 44.
[11] *Ibid.*, IV, 14, 42, for Agricola, Celsus, Amatus, and Mummolus, all patricians of Gallo-Roman origin. The patrician as a military commander should not be confused with the patrician who was governor of Marseilles (*ibid.*, IX, 22).

long after Sigulf, one of Sigibert's supporters, drove him out. Chilperic's son Theudebert was more successful: he took control of Tours, Poitiers, and other cities of Sigibert's south of the Loire. At Poitiers, Theudebert defeated Sigibert's Duke Gundobald, drove his army from the field, slaughtered a large number of the city's inhabitants, and compelled the city to submit to Chilperic. He then plundered the area around Limoges and Cahors.[12]

Sigibert did not immediately respond to Chilperic's attacks. In 574, however, he gathered a force of pagan Germans from beyond the Rhine and led them against his brother. Fearing the oncoming attack of Sigibert, Chilperic arranged a treaty with Guntram whereby the latter would stop Sigibert from crossing the Seine and reaching his territory. But by threatening to move against Burgundy, Sigibert pressured Guntram into allowing him to cross the Seine. Chilperic retreated before Sigibert's advance, refused to fight, and surrendered as the price for peace all that Theudebert had taken. Sigibert, however, had difficulty controlling the undisciplined warriors from beyond the Rhine and they plundered the inhabitants and churches of the Paris area.[13]

In the following year, Chilperic arranged another alliance with Guntram and moved his army against Sigibert, devastating his brother's territory up to Rheims. When Sigibert learned of Chilperic's advance, he again called upon trans-Rhenish fighting men and led them to Paris with Chilperic retreating before him. From Paris Sigibert ordered the counts of Châteaudun and Tours to lead their local levies against Theudebert. When the counts ignored his orders, he sent the Dukes Godegisel and Guntram Boso to call out the levies. They did so and moved against Theudebert, defeating his army and killing him. Guntram broke his alliance with Chilperic who, realizing that he could not stand alone in the field against Sigibert, retreated to Tournai where he prepared to withstand a siege. Sigibert's forces took Chilperic's territory west of Paris up to Rouen, where he was

---

[12] *Ibid.*, IV, 47.

[13] *Ibid.*, IV, 49: " . . . Sigyberthus rex gentes illas quae ultra Renum habentur commovit. . . ."

raised to the kingship of Chilperic's lands by the latter's erstwhile supporters. No sooner had this taken place, however, than two armed retainers of Queen Fredegund, wife of Chilperic, murdered Sigibert and wounded two of his followers, the Chamberlain Charegisel and the Goth Sigila. With this, the first phase of the *bella civilia* came to an end.[14]

This phase of the *bella civilia* amply illustrates the diversity of the units that formed the Merovingian military. Sigibert's main military support seems to have come from pagan Germans living beyond the Rhine. His Austrasian subjects had demonstrated during the reigns of his uncle Theuderic and his father, Chlotar, their unwillingness to obey their king and their dislike for fighting outside their own territory. Early in his own reign, they had further proved their ineffectiveness against the Avars. Sigibert found the Austrasians of little help in his wars with Chilperic, and this perhaps accounts for his inability to react to Chilperic's attacks before he had arranged for the support of trans-Rhenish troops in 574. It should be recalled that between 568 and 573 Chilperic attacked Sigibert's lands at least twice, but that the latter on his own made no counterattack before 574. In 570, however, Guntram had sent an army to recover for Sigibert what Chilperic had taken from him.

Sigibert's local levy of the Auvergne was loyal, but no match for a large army. As has already been mentioned, his counts at Tours and Châteaudun appear to have been disloyal and did not call up their levies when ordered to do so. These local levies only came into action when Sigibert provided them with new commanders. A Frank named Sigulf led a force in defense of Sigibert's cause at Bordeaux which proved to be of sufficient strength to drive out Prince Chlodovech's following; this force suggests a garrison which may have had its origin as a *centena* established in 508 by Clovis. Sigibert's troops in the Poitiers area, commanded by Duke Gundobald, were neither a local levy nor a popular militia. Rather, they may have been composed of Taifals who, as *laeti* established in the area, had been organized

[14] *Ibid.*, IV, 50, 51.

under a duke and integrated into the Merovingian military during the reign of Childebert, if not earlier.[15]

Sigibert's problems with the counts of Châteaudun and Tours amply demonstrate the necessity of having the loyal support of the magnates. The importance of loyal magnates to the function of royal power is further illustrated by what happened when Godinus, a follower of Sigibert, defected and joined King Chilperic, who gave him lands from the royal fisc. Gregory, who tells the story, notes that as a result Sigibert went to war against Chilperic. Godinus did not perform as had been expected of him while serving Chilperic in a military capacity, and therefore Chilperic deprived him of the lands previously granted to him and took his life as well. It may be wondered why Chilperic bought Godinus's support: Did Chilperic desire Godinus's loyalty for personal military service only, or because he was an important figure (one whose defection might cause a war) who led a personal armed following? Did he, for example, have a following like that of Titus who, as the leader of a band of *bucellarii*, was of such value that the Emperor Leo invited him to come to the East and made him a count? It seems reasonable to assume that Godinus was such a man, especially in light of the consequences of his defection and of Chilperic's willingness to buy his support with lands from the fisc. Men of military worth often may have received such grants. Mummolus received estates from the royal fisc to help support himself and his followers, as did Sigivald when he was ordered to hold the Auvergne for Theuderic.[16]

Chilperic seems to have operated with three field forces dur-

[15] On the garrison of Bordeaux see ch. I, n. 29. For the levies of Poitiers referred to by Gregory, *Hist.*, V, 26: ". . . Pictavi . . . ex iussu Chilperici regis abierunt"; VII, 2: "Berulfus vero dux cum . . . Pectavis. . . ."; and VI, 26: "Pectavis super se inruentibus. . . ." In IV, 47, Gregory makes a clear distinction between the people (*populus*) and Gundovald's force. On the Taifal connection see ch. I, n. 30, above.

[16] Gregory, *Hist.*, V, 3: "Godinus autem, qui a sorte Sigyberthi se ad Chilpericum transtulerat et multis ab eo muneribus locopletatus est, caput belli istius fuit; sed in campo victus, primus fuga dilabitur. Villas vero, quas ei rex a fisco in territurio Sessionico indulserat, abstulit et basilicae contulit beati Medardi. Ipse quoque Godinus non post multum tempus repentina morte praeventus, interiit." For Titus see ch. I, n. 45, and for Sigivald, ch. II, n. 6. On Mummolus's land see Gregory, *Hist.*, IV, 44: ". . . Macho villam

ing this period: one led by himself, another by his son Chlodo-vech, and a third by his son Theudebert. None of them seems to have been very large or very effective. Mummolus, Guntram's patrician, had little trouble defeating Theudebert's force, and Sigibert captured Theudebert when he was commanding a garrison at Soissons. Theudebert finally met his death at the hands of the local levies of Tours and Châteaudun. Sigibert's horde from beyond the Rhine did not find it difficult to discourage Chilperic from fighting, and Chlodovech was driven from Bordeaux by what may have been a garrison force led by Sigulf. Chilperic's Franks at Rouen in the western part of Gaul may perhaps have been a garrison or *centena* for that area. Unfortunately little can be ascertained with certainty about the composition of Chilperic's forces. They do not seem to have been local levies, but rather personal followings, such as that which Godinus probably had and the one which protected Queen Fredegund, known as *pueri reginae*.[17]

The reigns of the three Merovingian monarchs, Sigibert, Chilperic, and Guntram, from 561 to 575 amply demonstrate the importance of diverse military institutions to a ruler's success. Sigibert's Austrasian Franks were of little military value and he had to rely upon undisciplined hordes from beyond the Rhine. His local levies, however, in the old Gallo-Roman cities were effective. Chilperic, using private warbands, could gain brief successes but was not able to sustain his efforts against Sigibert's trans-Rhenish warriors or Guntram's disciplined Burgundian forces of Roman origin. The armies of the Burgundian kingdom, which owed much to imperial institutions, were the most successful during this period.

575–584

After the death of Sigibert at the hands of Queen Fredegund's armed retainers, Chilperic seems to have dominated military

---

Avennici territorii, quam Mummolus munere meruerat regio. . . ." See Bachrach, "Charles Martel," pp. 71–72.

[17] For the *pueri reginae* see Gregory, *Hist.*, VI, 32. On the *centena* of Rouen see Musset, *Les invasiones*, p. 187.

activity in Gaul. By early 576, Chilperic had taken Paris, captured Sigibert's widow, Queen Brunhild, and seized some of the dead king's treasure. Brunhild's infant son, Childebert, had been saved from his uncle in the preceding year by Duke Gundobald, who took him from Paris to Austrasia. There the boy was crowned king on Christmas day, 575. While Chilperic was at Paris, he sent Count Roccolen of Le Mans with the local levy of that city against Tours. This force ravaged the area, tried unsuccessfully to capture Guntram Boso (who had led the local levy of Tours victoriously against Theudebert earlier and who, after the death of Sigibert, took sanctuary with his family in the Church of St. Martin at Tours), but finally brought the city under Chilperic's control. As a part of his efforts to take possession of western Gaul, Chilperic ordered his son Merovech and Roccolen to take Poitiers. Merovech, however, disobeyed his father's orders and went to Tours where he spent Easter. Roccolen died late in February before accomplishing his task at Poitiers.[18]

The striking feature of these activities is that they were carried out in the dead of winter. It should be emphasized that they were not defensive actions but offensive campaigns designed for the conquest of western Gaul. The most effective force seems to have been the local levy of Le Mans, serving under Roccolen, but perhaps the most significant aspect of the situation was the complete inability of Childebert II's followers to organize some kind of effective defense.[19]

The disobedience of Merovech and the death of Roccolen slowed Chilperic's campaign, and he was soon to receive another blow. After Easter, Merovech went to Rouen where he married his aunt, Queen Brunhild, his father's enemy. When Chilperic learned of the marriage, he went to Rouen as quickly as possible, took Merovech into custody, and brought him to Soissons.[20]

---

[18] Gregory, *Hist.*, V, 1, 2, 4.

[19] Roccolen was at Tours during Epiphany which was in February of 576. He had been there for some time before that, having gone to Tours at about the same time Chilperic went to Paris. See n. 18 above.

[20] Gregory, *Hist.*, V, 2.

Brunhild had escaped to Austrasia. By this time (it was late spring or early summer of 576), at least some of the infant king's followers were ready to go into action. Duke Lupus of Champagne, a loyal supporter of Sigibert's house, seems to have been responsible for organizing a force of men from his territory to go against Soissons. They managed to drive Fredegund and Chlodovech out of the city, but Chilperic, who was camped not far from Soissons with an armed force, came to the rescue and decisively defeated the men of Champagne.[21]

After the Champagne offensive, Chilperic became convinced that Brunhild had turned Merovech against him and he had the prince tonsured and put into a monastery at Aninsula near Angers. At the same time, Chilperic sent Chlodovech to take Saintes, which belonged to Guntram. Saintes fell without noteworthy resistance, but Guntram retaliated by sending a force under Mummolus into the Limousin, which he devastated. Duke Desiderius, who moved against Mummolus, was defeated and barely escaped with his life.[22]

Practically nothing can be said with certainty about these forces which campaigned during the remainder of 576. It might be suggested that the force which attacked Soissons was a part of the levy of Champagne, a group whose activities are noted on several occasions by Gregory.[23] It may also be inferred that Mummolus led a part or all of the standing army of Burgundy, a force which has been discussed in some detail above (pp. 22–25). Chlodovech's troops may have been the local levies of Tours and Angers ("congregato exercitus, in terminum Toronicum et Andecavum").

In contrast to earlier campaigns, these later ones are curiously devoid of sieges. Perhaps the unsettled events following Sigibert's death created a situation in which his important followers were unsure whether to give their support to his son Childebert or to Chilperic. For example, Sigibert's referendary, Siggo, became a follower of Chilperic, but then switched his allegiance

[21] *Ibid.*, V, 3: ". . . collecti aliqui de Campania. . . ."
[22] *Ibid.*, V, 3, 13, 14.
[23] See n. 59 below.

to Childebert. In this crisis in allegiance there was a lack of strong commitment to defend Childebert II's cities against Chilperic's attacks — which would explain in part the lack of sieges during this time. Sigulf, who commanded Sigibert's garrison at Bordeaux, tried to seize control of the city for himself, but lost it to Chilperic's forces and then completely deserted Childebert's cause. This kind of tergiversation seems to have been reasonably common among Sigibert's erstwhile followers. Gregory also notes that Ciuciolo, Sigibert's former count of the palace, and Bishop Praetextatus, instead of supporting Childebert II, joined forces with Merovech who was a rallying point for magnates seeking a profitable connection.[24]

In late November or early December of 576, Merovech escaped from the monastery of Aninsula and went to Tours where he joined Guntram Boso. Each stayed in sanctuary at the Church of Tours with his armed followers. Count Leudast of Tours was foiled in his efforts to capture or kill them, though he did on one occasion manage to kill some of Guntram Boso's followers.[25] After spending about two months at Tours, Merovech and Guntram Boso left the city with some 500 men to go to Austrasia. Meanwhile, Chilperic learned that Merovech had taken sanctuary at the Church of Tours and ordered Gregory to cast him out. When the latter refused, Chilperic led an army against the city. This force, arriving after Merovech had departed, ravaged the area around Tours.[26]

While Merovech was passing through Auxerre in the dead of winter, presumably with his following, he was captured by King Guntram's Duke Herpo, but was released. Chilperic with his forces hunted throughout Champagne for his son but could not find him. Merovech joined Brunhild but was kept from remaining with her by the magnates of Austrasia; he then went into hiding in Champagne and remained there until some magnates of the Thérouanne area invited him to their territory, indicating that they preferred his rule to that of his father. But

[24] Gregory, *Hist.*, V, 2, 18; VII, 9.
[25] *Ibid.*, V, 14.
[26] *Ibid.*

when he arrived at the town of Thérouanne with a chosen group of his followers, they were surrounded in their quarters by a force of armed men who sent word to Chilperic that his son was trapped. Merovech realized the hopelessness of his position and ordered one of his followers, Gallien, to kill him; the rest were taken prisoner by Chilperic, who had them executed, some by torture.[27]

During the summer of 577 and before the death of Merovech, King Guntram and King Childebert II made a pact to stop Chilperic's conquest of their territories. In the autumn of the same year, Guntram Boso, apparently acting on his own, led a small group of his armed followers (*armati*) into Tours and, despite the opposition of the count, carried off his daughters from the church there and brought them to Poitiers.[28]

Shortly thereafter, Chilperic, undeterred by his brothers' alliance, attacked Poitiers, drove out Childebert II's garrison, deposed the count, and took control of the city. When Guntram Boso learned that Poitiers was under attack, he left his daughters at the Church of St. Hilary and fled from the city. The next year, on his way back to Poitiers to get his daughters, Guntram Boso encountered Chilperic's Duke Dragolen leading an armed force, and fighting ensued. Dragolen spurred his horse in a pell-mell charge against Guntram who unseated his opponent with a lance thrust to the throat. While Dragolen was hanging from his mount, one of Guntram's men killed him with a second lance thrust. Dragolen's followers were then put to flight and Guntram gathered up his daughters and went home.[29]

The activities of such magnates as Guntram Boso could cause no end of trouble for the monarchs. Perhaps this is best demonstrated by the career of Count Leudast of Tours. Gregory, who was Leudast's contemporary and neighbor, knew a great deal about him and discusses his activities in detail. Gregory's account of Leudast illustrates not only the relative power that a magnate might wield, but the diversity of the organization of armed force

[27] *Ibid.*, V, 14, 18.
[28] *Ibid.*, V, 17, 24, 25.
[29] *Ibid.*, V, 24, 25.

within the Merovingian kingdoms. Leudast became count of Tours during the reign of Charibert. When that king died and the city was supposed to pass under Sigibert's control, Leudast gave his support to Chilperic but lost his position as count. After gaining control of Tours, Chilperic restored the countship to Leudast, who, in this position, spent much of his time and effort in plundering and abusing the people whom he was charged to protect. Among those he maltreated were soldiers (*milites*) stationed in the city, perhaps because they owed their loyalty directly to the king.[30]

Leudast's activities eventually incurred the wrath of both Chilperic and Fredegund. When they deprived him of his courtship and determined to eliminate him, Leudast fled to Paris but continued to plot, causing suspicion to be thrown upon Bishop Gregory. Duke Berulf, who governed the territory of Tours and Poitiers, and Eunomius, the new count of Tours, posted guards (*custodes*) at the city gates, allegedly to watch Gregory. Meanwhile, Chilperic ordered that no one might receive Leudast into his house. Leudast returned to Tours, gathered up much of his treasure, and proceeded to Bourges, the possession of King Guntram. Chilperic's *pueri* pursued Leudast, but still he managed to avoid capture. At Bourges the count and a band of his armed followers robbed Leudast who barely escaped with his life. Leudast then rallied his followers, some of whom were from Tours, returned to Bourges, and retook part of his treasure. Berulf had learned of Leudast's activity and sent some of his own *pueri* to seize him. Leudast again escaped, this time to Poitiers where he took refuge at the Church of St. Hilary. From his sanctuary at St. Hilary, Leudast led his followers in plundering the people and property nearby. For these depredations he was expelled from the church. Shortly thereafter he went to Chilperic, who was camped with an army at Melun, to seek his pardon; then he traveled with the king to Paris to seek a pardon from the queen as well. She refused and sent her *pueri* to seize him.

[30] *Ibid.*, 47, 48: ". . . milites fustibus verberari. . . ."

Armed with swords and shields, they wounded and captured Leudast, who was first tortured and then executed.[31]

Among the armed forces which were operating during the episode described above was a band of *pueri regis* who pursued Leudast from Tours to Bourges, while the king himself was some two hundred miles to the north at Bernay. This force may be compared to one which Chilperic sent to Limoges a short time later. In March of 579, the people of Limoges attacked Chilperic's tax collectors who had to flee to save their lives. Chilperic, upon learning of this, sent a band of men from his side (*de latero suo*) to punish the inhabitants of Limoges. These men inflicted heavy losses on the people, killing many and exacting severe reprisals. These *pueri regis* further illustrate the diversity of Chilperic's forces as do the *milites*, stationed at Tours, who seem to have been responsible to an authority other than that of the count. This is suggested by Leudast's hostility toward them and by texts which indicate that *milites* served under a *tribunus*. A certain Medard served as *tribunus* at Tours at about that time. Also at Tours were men identified as *custodes*, who are apparently described by their function, although this may have been their title as well. It is reasonable to suggest that the *custodes* formed some kind of force other than a local levy, for Gregory speaks specifically of the local levy of Tours, but fails to indicate in any way that the *custodes* may have served in this same capacity. Gregory does mention that Chilperic used men called *custodes* to guard strategic positions such as the bridge across the Orge south of Paris. That local levies were not the only troops in some cities is illustrated by the *milites* at Tours and the distinction drawn by Gregory between these levies and the garrison at Poitiers.[32]

Like the magnates under previous Merovingian kings, many of Chilperic's important supporters—Duke Berulf and Duke

[31] *Ibid.*, V, 49; VI, 32.
[32] *Ibid.*, V, 28: "Unde multum molestus rex, dirigens de latere suo personas, inmensis damnis populum adflixit suppliciisque conteruit, morte multavit." On the *tribunus* see Gregory, *Hist.*, VII, 23, and ch. IV, pp. 78–80. Gregory, *Hist.*, VI, 19, for *custodes*; for the levy of Tours, IV, 50; V, 26; VI, 12, 31; and for the local levy and garrison at Poitiers, IV, 47; V, 24.

Dragolen among them—had bands of private armed retainers which were of crucial military importance. Gregory refers to Berulf's followers as "pueri" and to Dragolen's as "socii," suggesting the interchangeability of the terms. Childebert's Duke Guntram Boso had followers whom Gregory calls "armati" and "amici." Merovech also had a band of armed retainers which at one time, according to Gregory, numbered some 500 men. Among Merovech's following were important men like Sigibert's former count of the palace, and *pueri* like Gallien. If at the time Merovech and Guntram Boso left Tours together the latter can be considered Merovech's follower, it might be concluded that Merovech had at least one not so loyal supporter with his own armed band of retainers. The varied status of the men serving Merovech did not deter Gregory from calling them all — lower class *pueri* and magnates alike — *viri fortes*. The importance of these armed bands to a monarch, even a relatively successful one like Chilperic, is illustrated positively by the activities of Dragolen and Berulf, and negatively by the trouble which Merovech and Leudast caused the king.[33]

Local levies also played a significant role in royal attempts to win campaigns and gain power. For, like the personal armed followings, the local levies could be either beneficial or detrimental to the ruler who needed their support. It was not always easy to gain their loyalty because their leaders generally sought to serve on the winning side and could not always be counted upon to serve their king faithfully. In 579 Chilperic called up the local levies of Tours, Poitiers, Bayeux, Le Mans, and Angers to go against the Bretons. He also called up the Saxons of Bayeux, whose forebears had been settled in the area more than a century before by the Roman empire as military allies. The Saxons took severe losses in a sneak attack led by the Breton leader, Waroch. The Bretons nevertheless were forced to make peace rather than face Chilperic's full army of local levies reinforced by Saxon military colonists. As a result of this peace

[33] For Guntram see Gregory, *Hist.*, V, 24, 25; VI, 26. For Dracolen, V, 25; for Berulf, V, 49; and for Merovech, V, 14, 18.

Waroch swore fealty to Chilperic and gave him his son as a hostage.[34]

Chilperic's continued efforts to conquer western Gaul led him, in 581, to order Duke Desiderius to go against Guntram's cities in the southwest. Desiderius defeated Guntram's Duke Ragnovald and seized control of Agen, Périgueux, and Angoulême. While Desiderius was in the field against Guntram's forces, Chilperic's Duke Bladast attacked the Gascons, but was decisively defeated. Guntram planned to retaliate by sending the levy of Bourges against Tours, but Duke Berulf called out the local levy of Tours for defense of the city, and Guntram's forces made no permanent gains.[35] Two years after this successful defense of Tours, Chilperic again employed the levies in a two-pronged attack against Bourges, Guntram's stronghold in western Gaul. Duke Berulf, with the levies of Tours, Poitiers, Angers, and Nantes, attacked from the north, while Desiderius and Bladast with the forces from Chilperic's territory in southern Gaul attacked from the south. This army probably included the troops Desiderius had commanded when he conquered Guntram's cities two years earlier, the force Bladast had led against the Gascons, and perhaps the local levies of the cities of Agen, Périgueux, Saintes, Bordeaux, Toulouse, and Angoulême, which were all at that time under Chilperic's control. A bloody battle ensued between the local levy of Bourges and the force led by Desiderius and Bladast. Chilperic's army compelled the local forces to retreat and they took refuge in Bourges which Chilperic's dukes then put under siege.[36]

Meanwhile, Chilperic attacked and burned Guntram's stronghold at Melun. But Guntram, leading a force against his brother, defeated him decisively. Chilperic had to retreat to Paris and

[34] Ibid., V, 26: "Dehinc Toronici, Pictavi, Baiocassini, Caenomannici et Andecavi cum aliis multis in Brittania ex iussu Chilperici regis abierunt et contra Varocum . . . resedent. Sed ille dolose per nocte super Saxones Baiocassinos ruens, maximam exinde partem interfecit." Note Gregory's distinction between the men of Bayeux and the Saxons of Bayeux. For other references to these Saxons see X, 9, and Longnon, Géographie, pp. 172–175.

[35] Gregory, Hist., VI, 12. Longnon, Géographie, pp. 145ff.

[36] Gregory, Hist., VI, 31; IX, 31.

order his troops besieging Bourges to withdraw. For Guntram
to take the field in person was very unusual and both this action
and his failure to react sooner to Chilperic's attacks on his territory were probably due to his lack of a talented commander to
lead his forces, for Mummolus had defected to Childebert II.[37]

Although the most striking aspect of Chilperic's forces during
the campaign against Bourges is the considerable number of
local levies which were at his command when he needed them,
it should be noted that Chilperic could muster large forces without calling up the levies. For example, in the autumn of 584
Chilperic sent a military escort, which according to a contemporary numbered about 4000 armed men, to protect the im-
mense dowry that his daughter was taking on the road to Spain.[38]

While Chilperic was securing a more powerful position in
Gaul, his brother Guntram and his nephew Childebert II were
beset not only by his attacks, but by difficulties at home. After
Mummolus, Guntram's talented commander, switched his support
to Childebert, a group of Childebert's magnates, including Mummolus, arranged to support a pretender to Guntram's throne. In
582, with the aid of the Byzantine Emperor Tiberius, a certain
Gundovald, who had a long-standing but unaccepted claim to
royal blood, landed at Marseilles with a small following and a
large treasure. Leaving his treasure there, he obtained horses
from Bishop Theodore and joined Mummolus at Avignon. Guntram Boso, though a party to Gundovald's plot, went to Marseilles
where he arrested Theodore and seized the treasure. This altered
Gundovald's plans and he retreated to an island in the Mediterranean. Soon after, Guntram Boso was taken prisoner by King
Guntram's men and condemned for his part in bringing Gundovald to Gaul. In an effort to clear himself and save his family,
Guntram Boso promised to capture Mummolus. At the head of
the local levies of Velay and Auvergne, Guntram Boso advanced
on Avignon. Mummolus, however, arranged that all the boats
which might be used to take Guntram Boso and his troops across
the Rhone be hidden and that only unworthy craft be made

[37] *Ibid.*, VI, 31.
[38] *Ibid.*, VI, 42.

available. Thus when Guntram Boso and his men were in mid-stream, their boats began to fall apart and sink and many fighting men were lost in the river. This was not the only stratagem that Mummolus used to prepare for Guntram Boso's attack, for he also dug a moat on the eastern side of Avignon into which he directed water from the Rhone. To make the moat an even more formidable obstacle, deep pits were dug at random so that although at certain places an attacker might be able to wade, with his next step he might sink over his head. These tactics did not prevent Avignon from being besieged, although Guntram Boso nearly drowned in the treacherous pits in the moat and the life of a follower (*amicus*) of his was lost when his attempts to escape from a pit were foiled by his heavy armor. When Childebert II learned that two of his supporters, Guntram Boso and Mummulos, were thus engaged, he ordered Duke Gundulf to bring peace among the king's followers at Avignon, which he succeeded in doing.[39]

Although Childebert successfully prevented this incident from becoming a full-scale war, his youthfulness caused difficulties, as did the machinations of the magnates. Not only did many of them connive to bring Gundovald into Gaul, but some worked secretly for King Chilperic. Others overtly sought aggrandizement at their king's expense. Two such magnates, Ursio and Berthefred, with their followers, plundered the lands of Duke Lupus of Champagne, a loyal supporter of the king, and drove him out of his duchy despite the support he received from the royal house.[40]

Nonetheless, Childebert did enjoy a strong measure of support on at least one occasion from the rank and file (*minor populus*) of his forces. This occurred when Bishop Egidius of Rheims and some of Childebert's other magnates arranged a treaty with Chilperic and prevailed upon the youth to march in his uncle's support. The *minor populus* refused, however, saying that the king's magnates, who allowed his cities to be taken over and his people to be subjugated, were selling him out to

[39] *Ibid.*, VI, 1, 24, 26.
[40] *Ibid.*, X, 19; VI, 4.

Chilperic. The *minor populus* attacked Egidius, who barely escaped in a precipitous flight in which many of his followers (*socii*) fell along the way because their horses were exhausted. In 584 Childebert managed to secure sufficient support from his subjects (or perhaps from trans-Rhenish warriors) to muster an army large enough to invade Italy and obtain tribute from the Lombards. Such a lengthy and dangerous venture had not been undertaken by an Austrasian monarch since Theudebald's Italian campaign in 554.[41]

The uprising of the *minor populus* in Childebert's support as well as the successful expedition into Italy in 584 indicates that he did have some following, yet he was generally at the mercy of the magnates from his accession to the throne until the death of Chilperic in 584. Guntram, on the other hand, was in a considerably stronger position. The local levy of Bourges remained loyal to him, as did the standing army of Burgundy. Even without the capable leadership of Mummolus, this force under Guntram's personal command was able to defeat Chilperic's troops in the field.

Chilperic had dominated military affairs in Gaul after the death of his brother Sigibert, but when he attained the pinnacle of power and success, the same fate that had befallen his brother also became his: he was struck down by the hand of an assassin. This led to struggles that involved his lands and his erstwhile supporters. It should be pointed out that Chilperic had only been moderately successful when he relied essentially upon warbands between 561 and 575, but as he expanded his holdings into more Romanized and more urbanized areas between 575 and 584 and utilized local levies his cause prospered considerably more.

584–593

When the news of Chilperic's murder spread across the land, the magnates and monarchs began vying for power and support, resulting in conflicts that resembled the chaos following the death of Sigibert a decade earlier. Although a number of Chil-

[41] *Ibid.*, VI, 31, 42.

peric's adherents remained loyal to Queen Fredegund, and his son Chlotar II was even crowned king of Neustria, other supporters of Chilperic declared their allegiance to either Childebert II or the pretender Gundovald. The major conflict which flared up after Chilperic's death was not, however, a struggle for personal supporters, but a struggle for the deceased ruler's cities. Soon after his death, Childebert's Duke Gararic seized Limoges and Poitiers, the local levies of Blois and Orléans attacked Châteaudun, the men of Bourges subjected Tours to King Guntram's rule, and then together the levies of Bourges and Tours took Poitiers for Guntram. In this struggle for power and this vying for position, magnates led their armed bands in all kinds of activities: for example, Avius, who had been raiding and plundering in the area around Poitiers with his followers, was killed by Childeric the Saxon who at that time was leading his own armed retainers (*pueri*).[42]

Childebert and Guntram were not the only ones who hoped to gain by Chilperic's death, for Dukes Desiderius and Bladast joined Gundovald's cause. Desiderius, upon learning of his king's death, led a band of picked men into Toulouse and seized the treasure that Princess Rigunth had been taking to Spain. He placed the treasure under guard in Toulouse and sped to Avignon where he met Gundovald and Mummolus. In November of 584 Desiderius, Gundovald, Mummolus, and their retainers quickly moved to Brives-la-Gaillarde near Limoges, where Gundovald was raised to the kingship. Their plans to go north and occupy Poitiers were thwarted, however, by the levies of Orléans and Bourges which had retaken the city after the Poitivins returned to Childebert's side following their submission to the men of Bourges and Tours. Therefore Gundovald went south, receiving the submission of Angoulême, Périgueux, and Toulouse, and proceeded to Bordeaux. In January or early February of 585,

---

[42] For Chilperic's supporters defecting to Childebert see Gregory, *Hist.*, VII, 4; for Gundovald's supporters, VII, 9, 10, 27; for Duke Gararic, VII, 13; for the levies of Blois, Orléans, Châteaudun, and Chartres, VII, 2; for Bourges, VII, 12; for those of Chilperic's followers who remained loyal to his son, VII, 7; and VII, 3: " . . . unus ex pueris Childerici Avonem hasta transfixit."

when Guntram learned of Gundovald's activities in the south, he arranged a pact with Childebert and sent those troops previously ordered to Poitiers to seek out the pretender and capture him. Guntram's force, under the command of Duke Leudegisel and the patrician Aegilen moved south to the Dordogne River and waited there for news of Gundovald.[43]

Meanwhile, when Gundovald learned of Leudegisel's advance, he retreated rapidly toward the fortress of Convenae (modern Saint-Bertrand-de-Comminges). The remains of his treasure were being transported by camels; because they could not keep up with his retreating army, many were abandoned, as were horses exhausted by the rigorous pace. Realizing that a showdown with Guntram's forces was near at hand, Gundovald sent messengers to the magnates of Childebert's kingdom whose support he had been intending to buy with the great treasure he was bringing with him. His emissaries, however, were captured by Guntram's counts and were unable to carry out their mission. Early in February, probably before the twentieth, Gundovald made plans for the winter, gathering and storing provisions at Convenae, a hilltop fortress with an internal water supply. He then tricked the armed inhabitants of the fortress into leaving, relying upon the strength of his position and the ability of his supporters to hold out until the magnates of Childebert's kingdom and their followers came to his rescue.[44]

While Gundovald was in retreat, Leudegisel received word that the pretender had crossed the Garonne and was heading south, so he sent his cavalry in hot pursuit. Some of the men were drowned while crossing the Garonne, but those who survived found the exhausted horses and treasure-laden camels and thus picked up Gundovald's trail. When Leudegisel learned that Gundovald had reached Convenae, he ordered his slow-moving baggage train and infantry to converge on the fortress. He also commanded his horsemen to ride to Convenae with all possible

[43] Gregory, *Hist.*, VII, 9, 10, 24, 26, 27, 28, 31, 33, 34; VII, 24: "Anno igitur decimo Childeberthi regis rex Gunthramnus, commotis gentibus regni sui, magnus iuncxit exercitum. Sed pars maior cum Aurilianensibus adque Biturigis Pectavum petiit."
[44] *Ibid.*, VII, 30, 34.

speed, presumably to keep Gundovald from provisioning the fortress for a long siege. Fortunately for Gundovald, Leudegisel's cavalry stopped to plunder the Church of St. Vincent near Agen and did not carry out its mission.[45]

By the end of February or early March, all of Leudegisel's forces were finally encamped around Convenae with their tents pitched, their foragers in the field, and access to and from the fortress blocked. After some two weeks, Leudegisel found it necessary to prepare new siege engines; battering rams were mounted on wagons covered with sheds to protect the attackers from missiles hurled from the walls of the fortress. Leudegisel's troops also tried to fill up the moat on the eastern side of the fortress, but their efforts were to no avail. Each attempt to storm or breach the walls was met successfully by the defenders, who hurled down loads of stones and cauldrons of burning oil and pitch from the walls.[46]

Though Leudegisel's elaborate siege operations were unsuccessful, Convenae nevertheless fell to the attackers. When Mummolus and Gundovald's other supporters learned that help would not be forthcoming from the magnates of Childebert's kingdom, they concluded that their position was hopeless and in return for a promise of pardon from Leudegisel they pressured Gundovald into surrendering. The pretender, knowing he had been betrayed, had no choice but to surrender since the magnates' followers were the only troops he had. Perhaps if Gundovald had not tricked the resident fighting men of Convenae into leaving the fortress, he would have had a force capable of counteracting that of Leudegisel. At any rate, more was lost than the fortress, for despite assurances to the contrary, Gundovald, Mummolus, and

[45] *Ibid.*, VII, 35.

[46] *Ibid.*, VII, 35, 37: "Quintus et decimus in hac obsidione effulserat dies, et Leudeghiselus novas ad distruendam urbem machinas praeparabat. Plaustra enim cum arietibus, cletellis et axebus tecta, sub quae exercitus properaret ad distruendos muros. Sed cum adpropinquassent, ita lapidibus obruebantur, ut omnes adpropinquantes muro conruerint. Cupas cum pice et adipe accensas super eos proicientes, alias vero lapidibus plenas super eos deiciebant. Sed cum nox certamina prohiberit, hostes ad castra regressi sunt."

Bishop Sagittarius were killed. Some of the other magnates, however, managed to escape.[47]

Unlike Gundovald's army, Guntram's forces, described by Gregory as a huge army, were called out from throughout his kingdom and consisted of all those men who owed service. Not only were the fighting men of the old kingdom of Burgundy, under their patrician, Aegilen, called out, but so too were the local levies of many of Guntram's cities, such as Bourges, Poitiers, and Tours. Duke Leudegisel, the overall commander, had a substantial body of cavalry, presumably strong enough to keep Gundovald from provisioning Convenae and perhaps even large enough to engage the pretender's entire force if necessary. If these mounted troops were not thought capable of accomplishing at least the former, there seems to be no reason for their being sent in hot pursuit of the enemy. There is no way, however, to identify the role which these horsemen played within the organization of Leudegisel's forces. In addition to a cavalry force of note, Leudegisel's army carried a substantial quantity of matériel, including tents and probably siege engines. He also employed "engineers" capable of building and perhaps even designing siege engines.

The deaths of Chilperic and Gundovald and the pact between Childebert and Guntram ended the *bella civilia* for a time. Both kings now sought to subdue those magnates whose loyalty they questioned and to extend their efforts in the realm of foreign affairs. Childebert, for instance, sent armies into Italy on several occasions. Each effort, however, seems to have fared worse than the previous one. The only Italian campaign described in considerable detail is that which twenty dukes, serving under Childebert, led in 590. Part of their force included the levy of Champagne commanded by Wintrio, the duke of Champagne, and Audovald, who was also a duke. With six of the other dukes, Audovald moved on to Milan, but could find neither a Lombard army to fight nor the Byzantine army with which he was supposed to join. When Olo, another of these dukes, besieged Bel-

---

[47] *Ibid.*, VII, 30, 32, 36. For personal armed followings, VI, 20, VII, 38, IX, 35, and Bachrach, "Charles Martel," pp. 70–72. Gregory, *Hist.*, VII, 39.

linzona, he was killed and many of his men were cut down while foraging. In northwestern Italy Cedinus, with thirteen dukes, took at least five Lombard fortresses. In general, however, Childebert's troops were unable to coax a Lombard army into meeting them on the field, and the Merovingian forces were unable to subjugate any of the larger Lombard cities, such as Pavia. After ravaging northern Italy for some three months and being wracked by fever and disease, Childebert's army retreated into Gaul. Many of the soldiers were so poorly off that they had to sell their arms and other possessions in order to obtain food.[48]

In the spring of 585, immediately following the Gundovald affair, Guntram ordered the fighting forces of his entire kingdom against the Goths in Septimania. Men from north of the Saône, west of the Rhone, and north of the Seine, along with men of the old Burgundian kingdom, advanced on Nîmes, plundering all along the way, even in Guntram's own territory. The local levies of Bourges, Saintes, Périgueux, and Angoulême, Childebert's levy of Auvergne, and people from other cities in Guntram's kingdom moved on Carcassonne, also plundering as they traveled. Neither of these forces was able to take those Gothic cities which closed their gates. No effort was made to mount a siege; only the surrounding areas and the cities whose citizens were foolish enough to open their gates were plundered. By the end of July it became clear that this army was not going to subjugate Septimania; not only were Guntram's troops finding it difficult to forage, but the hostile populace was continually harassing them. By the middle of August when the campaign was over, many of the participants — Gregory says 5000 — had died of hunger or had been killed by the people in the areas they traversed.[49]

The failure of Guntram's forces in Septimania seems to have encouraged Reccared, the Visigoth king, to attack the Merovingian frontier. He plundered the area around Toulouse and raided up to the Rhone; he captured the garrisons of the fortress at

[48] *Ibid.*, VI, 42; VIII, 18, and Paul, *Hist.*, III, 29. Also Gregory, *Hist.*, X, 3: "Audovaldus vero dux cum Vinthrione, commoto Campaniae populo. . . ."
[49] Gregory, *Hist.*, VIII, 30.

Cabaret and Beaucaire, plundered within the walls, and then left them deserted. After accomplishing this, he shut himself up within the fortress of Nîmes. Learning of Reccared's raid, Guntram appointed Leudegisel as patrician in place of Aegilan. Leudegisel then proceeded with troops to regarrison the fortresses devastated by Reccared, while Duke Nicetius of Auvergne led a force to patrol the frontier.[50]

It is worth noting that even before the Burgundian kingdom had fallen under Merovingian rule, garrisoned fortresses played an important role in the defense of the area. Using erstwhile Roman fortifications and garrisons often descended from *laeti* and *milites*, the Burgundian monarchs and their Frankish successors provided for the protection of the frontiers, the imprisonment of enemy captives, and perhaps the bases for standing military forces. The fortresses attacked by Reccared and regarrisoned by Leudegisel were part of Guntram's frontier defenses, which probably included the fortified cities of Orange and Lodève before the latter fell into Gothic hands. The men called to regarrison the forts at Cabaret and Beaucaire served under the patrician and may perhaps have been detached from the Burgundian standing army. The men whom Duke Nicetius led to patrol the border of Childebert's kingdom were not of the levy of Auvergne, but *custodes* of some kind and perhaps a permanent military body.[51]

In 587 Duke Desiderius, who had become a supporter of King Guntram after Gundovald's death, and Count Austrovald of Toulouse, who served as his second in command, led the local levy of Toulouse against Carcassonne. The Gothic garrison at Carcassonne learned of the impending attack, however, and went out to meet Desiderius's force, but when the battle began the Goths turned and fled. Desiderius attacked their rear guard and pur-

[50] *Ibid.*, VIII, 30; IX, 7: "Unum etiam castro Ugernum nomen cum rebus atque habitatoribus desolantes, nullo resistenti, regressi sunt." This last attack was in 587, indicating that Beaucaire was regarrisoned by that time. For the Visigothic side of this campaign see Thompson, *The Goths in Spain*, pp. 92–94.

[51] V. *Epiphanii*, 171; Procopius, *H.W.*, V, xii, 29; xiii, 3; Gregory, *Hist.*, IV, 42. Also Longnon, *Géographie*, pp. 441, 613, and Thompson, *The Goths in Spain*, pp. 92–94.

sued it hotly, but when he reached the walls of the city only a few of his men were still with him; the others had been unable to keep up because their horses were exhausted. Seeing Desiderius's precarious position, the men of the city rushed out and killed the duke and most of those with him.[52]

Austrovald, who replaced Desiderius as duke in the area of Toulouse, later subjected Carcassonne to Guntram's control, but Guntram's desire to gain control of the Gothic-held cities in Septimania did not end with this victory. In 589, four years after his first futile attempt to subjugate Septimania, he again sent an army into the area, this time made up of the local levies of Périgueux, Bordeaux, Agen, and Toulouse. Duke Boso commanded the force, with a certain Antestius as second in command. Claudius, the Gothic leader in Septimania, prepared an ambush for Boso's levies. He sent a small force against the invaders' camp and kept the remainder of his men hidden some distance away. The small attacking force was easily repelled and as it retreated, Boso's men pursued it. Soon they found themselves between the two Gothic forces and the ensuing attack almost wiped them out. Boso's camp was taken and only those who were able to reach their mounts escaped; those less fortunate were either killed or captured.[53]

Guntram's efforts to gain control of Septimania were curtailed by these failures and also by his need to defend other parts of his kingdom against the Bretons who had been raiding in the west. In response to these raids, Guntram sent a force under Dukes Beppolen and Ebrachar. On this campaign Beppolen was to fall victim to Ebrachar's plotting and to Queen Fredegund's animosity. The queen ordered her Saxons from Bayeux to cut their hair in the Breton style and to join them as allies. While Beppolen was fighting against both the Bretons and the Saxons, Ebrachar retreated with the larger part of the force, leaving his colleague at the mercy of the enemy who murdered him and his personal followers in the swamps. Learning that Beppolen was dead, Eb-

[52] Gregory, *Hist.*, VIII, 45.
[53] *Ibid.*, IX, 31; John Biclar, *Chron.*, 589; Fred., IV, 10. Bachrach, "Feigned Retreat," p. 266.

rachar returned and made peace with the Breton leader. But to return to their own territory Ebrachar's forces had to cross the Vilaine River. The mounted troops were able to swim their horses across the river, but the less important fighting men (*inferiores* and *pauperes*), who were on foot, were not as successful. Some tried to swim across on the backs of horses (*caballi*) from the baggage train, but most of the untrained mounts and their equally unskilled riders were drowned. Those who were not drowned but remained on the west bank of the river were either killed or captured by the Bretons who thus broke the peace.[54]

Aside from these major military campaigns during the last decade of Guntram's life, there were many relatively minor encounters involving smaller groups. Guntram himself, according to Gregory of Tours, never went anywhere, even to church, without a large following of armed men. He also sent men from the court to carry out paramilitary missions, one of which was the killing of a certain Boantus by a detachment of *pueri* because he had been unfaithful to Guntram. Two of the more important men who served the king in this capacity were Antestius and Claudius; neither seems to have had an official title, but both led missions of a military nature from the court. As has already been mentioned, Antestius acted as second in command to Duke Boso in the campaign of 589; he also served Guntram by punishing troublemakers of Angers and Nantes. Claudius, too, took part in such activities; his service cost him his life. He was sent with his own *pueri* to capture Eberulf, one of Chilperic's high officials accused of his murder. Claudius and his *pueri* fought it out with Eberulf and his followers, resulting in the death of both leaders and some of the *pueri*.[55]

Many of these paramilitary activities were directed against Childebert, who not only had to deal with such minor harassments but was faced with a more serious conspiracy. For in the autumn of 587 three of his magnates — Berthefred and the Dukes

---

[54] Gregory, *Hist.*, X, 9.

[55] *Ibid.*, VII, 8, 18; IX, 3, for Guntram's personal guards; VIII, 11, for Boantus; VIII, 43; IX, 31, for Antestius; and VII, 29, for Claudius.

Rauching and Ursio — plotted to kill the king and then rule the kingdom in the names of his sons. Childebert learned of the plot, however, and invited Rauching to the court where the king had the duke murdered. At the same time, Childebert sent some of his *pueri* from the court to seize Rauching's extensive estates. When the *pueri* who had accompanied Rauching to the court learned of their lord's death, one of them rode off with word of the disaster to his widow who received the news as she was parading through the streets of Soissons with a following of her own armed guards.[56] While Rauching went to see Childebert, Ursio and Berthefred prepared their forces. When they learned of Rauching's death, they took refuge with their followers and families at a Roman fortification which had been converted into a church. In December of 587 Childebert sent a force against them. Godegisel, Childebert's commander on this occasion, laid siege to the fortified place and then tried to burn out the conspirators. Ursio sallied forth with his followers and cut down many of the besiegers before he himself was killed. Berthefred escaped on horseback with some of his armed retainers, but they were eventually caught and slain.[57]

MILITARY COMPLEXITY: 561–593

The period during which one or more of Clovis's grandsons ruled in Gaul is the most thoroughly documented era in Merovingian history. Because of the comparative abundance of evidence, the heterogeneous nature of the Merovingian military can be demonstrated in considerable detail. One of the most important innovations by the Merovingian monarchs, which contributed to the complexity and diversity of their military organization, was the development of local levies in many of the cities in Gaul.

These local levies, either acting singly or in groups, played a significant role in military affairs. The value of these levies to the king depended in part on his ability to hold the loyalty of the important men who commanded them, as is illustrated by Sigibert when he had to send loyal commanders to get the levies of Châ-

---

[56] *Ibid.*, IX, 9.
[57] *Ibid.*, IX, 12.

teaudun and Tours to support him in 575. His son Childebert found it difficult during the first decade of his reign to keep the loyalty of his magnates and was therefore unable to use the local levies of his cities effectively. Similarly, King Guntram had trouble with his magnates during the last years of his conflict with Chilperic and consequently had difficulty in mobilizing the support of his own local levies. Conversely, Chilperic utilized the local levies of his cities effectively in his expansion at the height of his power because he had the support of his commanders.

It was only in cities in Neustria and Aquitaine that the locally based levies appeared during the reigns of Clovis's grandsons. Gregory notes their operation, between 568 and 591, at Agen, Angers, Angoulême, Auvergne, Bayeux, Blois, Bordeaux, Bourges, Chartres, Châteaudun, Le Mans, Nantes, Orléans, Périgueux, Poitiers, Saintes, Toulouse, Tours, and Velay.[58] In Champagne a levy seems to have been organized on a provincial basis, rather

---

[58] *Ibid.*, IV, 30: "Sigyberthus vero rex Arelatinsim urbem capere cupiens, Arvernus commovere praecipit. Erat enim tunc Firminus comes urbis illius, qui cum ipsis in capito abiit." IV, 50: "Dolorem enim ingerit animo ista civilia bella referre. . . . Sigyberthus . . . mittens nuntius Dunensibus et Toronicis, ut contra Theodoberthum ire deberent." V, 1: "Tunc Roccolenus cum Cinomannicis Toronus venit et praedas egit et multa scelera fecit. . . ." V, 26: "Dehinc Toronici, Pictavi, Baiocassini, Caenomannici et Andeacavi . . . ex iussu Chilperici regis abierunt et contra Varocum . . . ad Vicinonam fluviam resedent." VI, 12: "Berulfus vero dux, cum Bitorigus musitare, quod Toronicum terminum ingrederentur, audisset, exercitum commovet et se in ipsos fines statuit." VI, 26: "At ille, adsumptos secum Arvernis atque Villavis, Avennione abiit." VI, 31: "Berulfus vero dux cum Toronicis, Pectavis, Andecavisque atque Namneticis ad terminum Bitoricum venit." VII, 2: "Aurilianensis cum Blesensibus iuncti super Dunenses inruunt eosque inopinantes prosterunt. . . . Quibus discedentibus, coniuncti Dunenses cum reliquis Carnotenis. . . ." VII, 13: ". . . exercitum contra Pectavos commovit, ut scilicet ab una parte Toronici, ab alia Biturigi commoti cuncta vastarent." VII, 21: "Tunc data occasione, ut custodiretur, Aurilianensis atque Blesensis vicessim ad has excubias veniebant, impletisque quindecim diebus, cum praeda multa revertebantur, adducentis iumenta, pecora, vel quodcumque derepere potuissent." VII, 24: "Sed pars maior cum Aurilianensibus adque Biturigis Pectavum petii." VIII, 30: "Similiter et Byturigi, Sanctonici cum Petrocoricis, Ecolesenensibus vel reliquarum urbium populum. . . . usque Carcasonam urbem devicti, similia mala gesserunt. . . . Tunc et Nicetius dux cum Arvernis in haec expeditione commotus, cum reliquis urbis adsedit." IX, 31: ". . . ipse cum Sanctonicis, Petrocoricis Burdegalensibusque, Agennensibus etiam ac Tolosanis illuc direxit."

than on the more limited scope of the other local levies.[59] In neither Austrasia nor the lands which before 534 formed the Burgundian kingdom do locally organized levies seem to have been developed during this period. Gregory makes no mention of forces at Cologne, Zulpich, Metz, Mainz, Verdun, Strasbourg, Worms, Spire, Toul, or Maastricht in a manner which might be interpreted as a force organized on a local basis. Neither does Gregory mention levies at Lyons, Nevers, Autun, Châlons, Geneva, Grenoble, or Valence. It is true that Gregory lived at Tours and perhaps showed a greater interest in the western and more Roman parts of Gaul than in Austrasia and Burgundy. Yet Lyons and Vienne are closer to Tours than either Toulouse or Bordeaux, both of which Gregory indicates as having a local levy; and it would be difficult to argue that the latter were more Romanized than the former. In addition, it must be noted that among the dozens of military encounters which Gregory describes many involved forces from Austrasia and the erstwhile Burgundian kingdom.

The levy of a city was usually commanded by the count of the *civitas*, although in several instances a group of cities, with their counts, was brought together under the overall administrative and military control of a duke. For example, Duke Ennodius was responsible for Tours, Poitiers, Aire, and Lescar; Duke Berulf was his predecessor in Tours and Poitiers; Nicetius was the duke of Clermont, Rodez, and Uzes; Duke Beppolen administered the cities of western Gaul belonging to Chlotar II, but controlled by King Guntram. To these commands might be added the regional levy of Champagne which was led by the duke. These dukes who served as the administrative and military heads of several cities should be differentiated from those dukes who held ad hoc command of one or more local levies for a single campaign. For example, Duke Guntram Boso took command of the levies of Auvergne and Velay in 582 in an attempt to rout Mummolus who was ensconced at Avignon, and Duke Boso (not

[59] *Ibid.*, V, 3: ". . . collecti aliqui de Campania. . . ." X, 3: "Audovaldus vero dux cum Vinthrione commoto Campaniae populo. . . ." X, 27: "Commotus autem pro hac causa Campanensis populus. . . ."

to be confused with the former) commanded the levies of Périgueux, Bordeaux, Agen, and Toulouse in 589 for an invasion of
Septimania.[60]

During the latter part of the sixth century, these locally organized levies, as well as the provincial levy of Champagne,
were used in both offensive and defensive actions. As defensive
measures they protected their area from invasion and performed
police duties of a substantial nature. Offensively, levies went
against the Goths in Septimania, the pretender Gundovald, and
the Bretons. None of the city levies were used outside of Gaul,
however; they did not go south of the Alps, south of the Pyrenees, or east of the Rhine. In fact, ventures of more than 300
miles from their home base seem to have been beyond their competence, although they did remain away for more than three
months at a time during all seasons.[61]

The personnel composition of these levies is difficult to ascertain. Neither all men, nor even all freemen, were required to
serve. For example, on occasion a son might ask and receive permission to serve in place of his father, who would owe service,
whereas the son, who was in some cases more fit to serve, did
not.[62] The selective nature of the local levy is further emphasized
by an episode which took place in Guntram's army when it went
against the pretender Gundovald during the autumn of 584. In
addition to the levy of Tours, a large number of other inhabitants of the city (whom Gregory clearly distinguishes from the
levy) followed along in the hope of obtaining booty.[63]

[60] *Ibid.*, VI, 18, 21, 26, 31, 42; IX, 31.

[61] The levy of Poitiers which traveled south to fight at Convenae in 585
seems to have gone further from its home base than any of the other local
levies. The provincial levy of Champagne went beyond the borders of Gaul
and fought in Italy (Gregory, *Hist.*, X, 3).

[62] *Form. Andec.*, 37 (*MGH Form. Merov. et Karol.*): "Dum in omnibus
et per omnia et super totum nobis fidiliter servire videras, multa penurias et
iniurias per deversa loca pro nostra necessitate successisti, et in utilitate
domnorum partibus Brittanici seu Wasconici austiliter ordine ad specie mea
fuisti, proinde convenit nobis, ut aliquid de facultatis nostra te emeliorare
deberent; quod ita et fecerunt." See the discussion of this by Boutaric,
Institutions militaires de la France, p. 59, and N. D. Fustel de Coulanges,
Histoire des institutions politiques de l'ancienne France (Paris, 1888), IV,
293, n. 2.

[63] Gregory, *Hist.*, VII, 28: "Post haec [autem] exercitus ab urbe Pectava

Any suggestion that service in the levies was universal is cast in doubt by the eloquent silence of the Frankish law codes on this point. These codes were drawn up and revised throughout the sixth century and do not mention an obligation for all to serve. At one time in the sixth century, however, both poor men and economic dependents seem to have been included among those who owed service in the local levies. But by the last quarter of that century it was customary, at least in northwestern Gaul, for the poor to be exempt from such service. Some economic dependents (particularly those of the Church of St. Martin) were exempt as well.[64] These exemptions were granted not out of benevolence, however, but rather because of the economic repercussions that would have resulted from the use of such people in the local levies. For economic dependents, burdened with labor services which they owed to their lords as well as with the upkeep of their own holdings, could hardly perform in even the most limited offensive campaigns (a week or two) without causing economic dislocations more damaging than their absence from military campaigning. Fields left unplanted or crops left to rot unharvested could not possibly have been permitted as an institutionalized consequence of the mode of military organization which flourished in Neustria and Aquitaine for a generation and more. In short, the demands of the division of labor caused certain limitations in the recruitment of men for the local levies. Whereas the requirements of economic dependence limited mobility and thus service, poverty had similar effects. The men who served in these local levies seem to have had to rely upon their own resources to provide the food and matériel necessary for their service. The inability of the poor to provide their own weapons and sustenance for several months of campaigning may well have been the reason for their eventual exclusion from the local levies.

remotus inantea post Gundovaldum profiscitur. Secutique sunt eum de Toronici multi lucri causa; sed Pectavis super se inruentibus, nonnulli interempti, plurimi vero spoliati redierunt. Hi autem qui de his ad exercitu prius iuncxerant pariter abierunt."

[64] *Ibid.*, V, 26: "Post haec Chilpericus rex de pauperibus et iunioribus eclesiae vel basilicae bannos iussit exigi, pro eo quod in exercitu non

In negative terms, it has been ascertained that the personnel of the local levy was not the same as all the male or the free male inhabitants of the *civitas,* and that both the poor and economic dependents were exempted. In positive terms, it seems reasonable to assume that the lowest possible economic status from which local levies might be recruited regularly were owners or holders of land with a sufficient number of economic dependents or slaves to perform the necessary agrarian services so that production would not suffer. This conclusion is supported by the conflict between the demands of the agricultural cycle and the logistical demands on an individual in a local levy. If the rank and file of the local levy were small landholders with a few slaves or economic dependents, it was also true that important personages (*magni viri*) served in the local levy, as can be demonstrated by the one from Auvergne.[65]

The Arvernian levy led by Firminus in 568 seems to have consisted, at least in part, of horsemen wearing helmets and carrying shields. Two difficulties arise, however, in drawing this conclusion from Gregory's account. Gregory uses a quotation from Virgil — "scuta virorum galeasque et fortia corpora volvit" — to indicate that they used helmet and shield. By using a quotation from Virgil, Gregory's remarks about the helmets and shields are less reliable than they would have been if he had used his own words. An even greater problem exists when attempting to ascertain if the levy of the Auvergne was mounted and had helmets and shields, because not only the levy but Audovar's troops were involved in this encounter.

Gregory's remarks concerning horses and armor therefore may refer to Audovar's group which was not even a local levy let

ambulassent. Non enim erat consuetudo, ut hi ullam exsolverent publicam functionem." VII, 42: "Post haec edictum a iudicibus datum est, ut qui in hac expeditione tardi fuerant damnarentur. Biturigum quoque comes misit pueros suos, ut in domo beati Martini, quae in hoc termino sita est, huiusmodi homines spoliare deberent. Sed agens domus illius resistere fortiter coepit, dicens: 'Sancti Martini homines hii sunt. Nihil eis quicquam inferatis iniuriae, quia non habuerunt consuetudinem in talibus causis abire.'"

[65] *Ibid.,* IV, 30, quoted in n. 58. The origins of this levy may go back to the Visigothic period when the men of the Auvergne, including some of the more important people, served at Vouillé (Gregory, *Hist.,* II, 37). R. Latouche, *The Birth of the Western Economy* (London, 1961), pp. 59–116.

alone a part of the levy of Auvergne. There are other instances of levies serving in armies with strong mounted contingents: the levies of Bourges and Poitiers served in Leudegisel's army which had a substantial force of horsemen; the force led by Desiderius against Carcassonne in 587 included the levy of Toulouse and had enough horsemen to rout the rear guard of the Gothic garrison; and the force commanded by Duke Boso in 589 when he attacked Septimania included the levies of Périgueux, Agen, Bordeaux, and Toulouse and had a noteworthy number of horsemen.[66] The ambiguity of the evidence is such that it is not possible to conclude positively that substantial elements in these local levies served on horseback and had armor. Nevertheless, the frequent mention of mounted forces in the same context with levies does make such a conclusion reasonable.

At times the Merovingian kings supplemented their forces with what might be called a general levy, including apparently just about anyone who could hurl a stone or swing a club. Among the terms used by Gregory to describe members of such levies are *inferiores* and *pauperes*. The military value of these elements seems to have been negligible and they do not seem to have seen very much action. The term *minor populus*, on the other hand, appears to refer to a stratum of society above that of the *inferiores* and *pauperes*. The *minor populus* was inferior to the magnates, and it may have formed the rank and file of the city levies.[67]

The general levies, though infrequently used, and the local levies can both be best described as a militia of sorts, a part-time army. In contrast, there were standing forces such as the patrician's army in Burgundy, the *laeti* and *milites* who served in garrisons, the erstwhile Roman allies like the Saxons who lived in colonies, and the *antrustiones* who served in part in the *centenae*. The *custodes* frequently mentioned by Gregory may have been

[66] Gregory, *Hist.*, IV, 38, for the Auvergne; VII, 35, for Leudegisel; VIII, 45, for Desiderius; and IX, 31, for Boso.

[67] *Ibid.*, VII, 24: ". . . rex Gunthramnus, commotis gentibus regni sui. . . ." VIII, 30: ". . . commoto omni exercitu regni sui, illuc dirigit. . . ." X, 9: ". . . inferiores et pauperes, qui cum his erant, simul transire non potuerunt." On the *minor populus* see VI, 31.

organized in special groups of some kind or they may have been drawn from one of the other standing forces. The contexts in which they are mentioned make it clear that they are not local levies. Most of these standing forces seem to be overwhelmingly imperial in origin — the *laeti* were Roman military colonists, the *milites* were descendants of Roman soldiers, the *centena* was commanded by a *centenarius* who held a Roman title. The *centena* was placed on lands of the royal fisc which was often the former imperial fisc. The *antrustiones* who served on the *centenae* were drawn not only from among the Franks, but from among the Romans and *laeti* as well. Those who served in garrisons performed their duties in fortified places built by the empire.

Along with these local and general levies, the Merovingian monarch had at his disposal a personal armed following which served him at the court. These fighting men were employed to quell minor uprisings, deal with unfaithful magnates, and of course to protect the king. Most often the rank and file of these groups are called *pueri*, which seems to indicate low estate. *Pueri*, nevertheless, were members of the royal *trust* and served as *antrustiones*.

As has already been mentioned in chapters I and II, the personal armed followings of the magnates also played an important role in the complex Merovingian military. The shifting loyalty of these powerful men could result in critical situations such as the Gundovald affair, Rauching's conspiracy, and Merovech's venture. In recognition of the problem caused by the shifting loyalty of these magnates, whom Gregory sometimes calls *leudes*, Guntram and Childebert II agreed not to "invite" each other's *leudes* to join them and not to accept those who volunteered to switch sides.[68] The example of Godinus, whose defection from Sigibert to Chilperic in exchange for lands from the Neustrian fisc caused a war between the two monarchs, is worth recalling in this context.

[68] *Ibid.*, IX, 20, for the *Pact of Andelot*: "Similiter convenit, ut nullus alterius leudis nec sollicitet nec venientes expipiat."

CLOVIS'S GRANDSONS

On the whole, the Merovingian military in the era of Clovis's grandsons is a confusing mosaic of heterogeneous elements. The legacy of imperial institutions — *milites, laeti,* allies, and garrisoned Roman fortifications — coexists with pagan hordes from beyond the Rhine, *centenae* of *antrustiones* recruited among Romans and barbarians, local levies from the cities of the Romanized parts of Gaul, the personal followings of the magnates, and the *pueri regis.* When a monarch was able and fortunate, these various groups tended to serve him with a significant measure of loyalty, but during minorities, regencies, and interregna, or other times of great stress and upheaval, many of these groups served nonroyal interests. The monarchs' struggle to maintain royal power cannot be separated from their efforts to control these many elements of the Merovingian military. Such efforts were constant and costly and the loyalty of the magnates, which was perhaps most important, was often for sale to the highest bidder.

CHAPTER IV

The Last of the Ruling Merovingians: 593-638

THE PERIOD of the last ruling Merovingians witnessed internal fighting similar to that which had characterized the reigns of Clovis's grandsons. Soon after the death of King Guntram in 593, some of the magnates of Childebert II's kingdom attempted to despoil Chlotar II's holdings since the young king no longer had the strong hand of Guntram to protect him and his lands. The first phase of this effort — undertaken by Duke Wintrio of Champagne and magnates (*superiores*) from Austrasia and Burgundy — was directed against Soissons. The force was neither a general levy nor the territorial levy of Champagne.[1]

When Queen Fredegund learned of Wintrio's maneuvers, she called together a number of dukes (*duces*) to decide what should be done to prevent Wintrio's men from seizing part of Chlotar's territory. (The word *dux*, as used here by the author of the *Liber Historiae Francorum*, seems to mean, in a nontechnical sense, simply the leader of a band of men.) The force which went to deal with Wintrio was led by Fredegund and Landri, mayor of the palace of Neustria, and was neither a general levy nor a local one as can be discerned from the terms used to describe it.[2]

[1] For the terms used to designate the levy of Champagne see ch. III, n. 59, above. *L.H.F.*, ch. 36.

[2] Longnon, *Géographie*, pl. X, for the cities held by Chlotar, and ch. III, n. 58, for the local levies in Gaul. See also Eugen Ewig, "Die fränkischen Teilreiche im 7 Jahrhundert (613–714)," *Trierer Zeitschrift*, XXII (1953), 86–105. See also ch. III, n. 60, above.

74

As a general stratagem for the battle, the queen suggested a surprise attack to compensate for her forces' weaknesses and to lessen the chances of an open battle, which would have placed her men at a severe disadvantage. In accordance with this plan, the Neustrian horsemen slowly advanced toward Wintrio's camp in the predawn behind a line of warriors carrying tree branches to camouflage their movements. The author of the *Liber*, who has described these events in considerable detail, contends that one of Wintrio's sentries heard the tinkle of a horse's bell and upon seeing the camouflaged horsemen, thought a forest had appeared where none had been before. When he mentioned the incident to his fellow sentry, he was told the bells belonged to their own mounts pastured near the camp and, as for his remark about the forest, he must be drunk his colleague concluded. In any event, a warning was not given; at dawn the Neustrians charged into Wintrio's camp killing a large number of men and scattering the rest. The Neustrians then took Rheims and ravaged Champagne before returning to Soissons with their booty.[3]

Although Childebert's prestige may have been diminished by the failure of his supporters, he was able to crush a Thuringian revolt in 595, suggesting that his army had recovered from the disaster two years earlier. He died soon after, however, and his sons Theuderic and Theudebert inherited his kingdom, receiving Burgundy and Austrasia, respectively. Soon after Childebert's death, Chlotar took over Paris and several other cities belonging to his cousins. In retaliation Theudebert and Theuderic led a force against the Neustrian kingdom, but Chlotar's followers were victorious once again, this time at Laffaux near Soissons. Little is known about this battle except that the Neustrians won with a charge.[4]

[3] *L.H.F.*, ch. 36: "Burgundiones et Austrasii superiores Franci simul commoti grande exercitu, valde Campanias digressi, paygo Suessionico cum Gundoaldo et Wintrione patriciis vastantes ingrediuntur. Haec audiens Fredegundis, cum Landerico et reliquos Francorum duces hostem congregat. Brinnacum villa veniens, multa dona et munera Francis ditavit, eosque ad pugnandum contra inimicos eorum coortans." See Fred., IV, 14. Fredegar and the *Liber* use the term *patrician* to describe both Wintrio and Gundoald. Gregory called the leader in Champagne a duke.

[4] *L.H.F.*, ch. 37, confuses two campaigns, one in the year 596 or 597

However, Theuderic and Theudebert had extensive military resources to draw on, and when fully exploited, these would place the less fortunate Chlotar at the brothers' mercy. Not only were the combined kingdoms of Theudebert and Theuderic more than three times larger than Chlotar's holdings, but the latter had only one local levy at his command — that of Bayeux. Theuderic could call on the levies of Toulouse, Agen, Nantes, Angers, Saintes, Angoulême, Périgueux, Orléans, Blois, Chartres, and Le Mans, as well as the standing army of Burgundy. Theudebert controlled the territorial levy of Champagne and the local levies of the Auvergne, Poitiers, Tours, Vellay, Bordeaux, and Châteaudun; he also had access to the general levy of Austrasia, pagan Germans from beyond the Rhine, and Alamans from the Transjura area.[5]

Despite this significant military advantage, it took the brothers more than four years to mobilize their superior forces and defeat Chlotar. In 600 Theuderic and Theudebert invaded Chlotar's kingdom and massacred his men on the banks of the Orvanne near Dormelles. They followed up this victory by attacking the towns along the Seine which Chlotar previously had conquered. The brothers' army cut gaping holes in the walls of the towns, carried off a large number of the populace, and devastated the area. Chlotar was so decisively defeated that his sole option was to surrender most of his territory; he was left with only twelve *pagi* between the Seine, the Oise, and the sea.[6]

Theudebert and Theuderic, two years after their triumph over Chlotar, conducted a successful invasion of Gascony, concerning which there is no information.[7] In the winter of 605 Theuderic fought against a force under the nominal leadership of Merovech, Chlotar's son; the real commander, however, was Landri. This campaign began in the autumn of 604 when Bertoald, mayor of

and the other in 600. Fred., IV, 17, treats the former. For Childebert see Fred., IV, 15, 16.
   [5] Longnon, *Géographie*, pl. X, and the last section of ch. III above.
   [6] Fred., IV, 20, and Longnon, *Géographie*, pl. X. *L.H.F.*, ch. 37, indicates that Theuderic leading a "hoste maximo ex Burgundia" defeated Chlotar's "commoto Francorum exercitu."
   [7] Fred., IV, 21.

THE LAST OF THE RULING MEROVINGIANS

the palace for Burgundy, set out with a following of 300 men to inspect the royal domains along the Seine (from Paris to the Channel) which Theuderic had recently taken from Chlotar. At Arèle, on the Seine not far from the coast, Bertoald stopped to do some hunting. When Chlotar learned where Bertoald was, he sent Merovech and Landri against him. Bertoald fled south to Orléans, and the Neustrians laid siege to the city. It was then almost mid-November and the siege was soon raised. Theuderic learned that Chlotar's forces were in the field and moved against them toward the end of December. Bertoald and his followers, in the van of Theuderic's army, were killed by Landri's men when they advanced too far beyond the main body of troops. Theuderic, however, was victorious; his troops captured Merovech, but Landri managed to escape. Although Theudebert and Chlotar confronted each other at Compiègne, peace was negotiated and both armies returned home without fighting.[8]

In the next year Theuderic decided to go to war against his brother Theudebert. The important men (*leudes*) of Theuderic's kingdom were not anxious to fight, however, and while some of them kept Theuderic occupied in conversation, a number of warriors murdered Protadius, the mayor of the palace, who had encouraged the war. As a result of this setback, Theuderic consented to make peace with his brother. This incident indicates once again the great power the magnates exercised in military activities.[9]

In 609 Theuderic, at the urging of his mother, Brunhild, ordered the Irish missionary Columbanus to leave his kingdom. Columbanus was driven out of his monastery at Luxeuil by

[8] *Ibid.*, IV, 25; Longnon, *Géographie*, pl. X; and F. Lot, *L'Impôt foncier et la capitation personelle* (Paris, 1928), p. 102.

[9] Fred., IV, 27: "Quod cum loco nomen Caratiaco Teudericus cum exercito castra metasset ortabatur a leudibus suis ut cum Theudeberto pacem iniret. Protadius singulos ortabatur ut prilium committeretur. . . . Protadius in tenturio Teuderici regis cum Petro archyatro tabulam ludens sedebat. Cum eum undique iam exercitus circumdasset et Teudericum leudis suae tenebat ne illuc adgrederit. . . . Inruentes super eum, tenturium regis gladio undique incidentis, Protadium interficiunt. Teudericus confusus et coactus cum fratri Theudeberto pacem inivit et inlesus uterque exercitus revertit ad propriis sedibus."

77

Baudulf, one of Theuderic's magnates, and was taken to Besançon. While in exile there, he helped a group of captives escape from Theuderic's prison. The *tribunus* who commanded a garrison of *milites* in the city tried to recapture the fugitives but was unsuccessful. Soon after, Columbanus himself escaped from Besançon and returned to his monastery. Theuderic, upon learning of these events, sent a troop of soldiers to the monastery to capture Columbanus, but they failed. Theuderic therefore ordered a band of men from the court under the leadership of Count Berthar and the magnate Baudulf to take Columbanus prisoner. When the missionary refused to come out from the monastery, Berthar and Baudulf departed; they left behind a group of men who dragged Columbanus from his sanctuary, and then a certain Ragamund in command of a troop of *custodes* escorted the monk from Theuderic's kingdom.[10]

The journey into exile undertaken by Ragamund and Columbanus provides some insights into communications and paramilitary transport during this period. Since Ragamund intended to travel from Luxeuil north and west to the mouth of the Seine, where Columbanus would sail to Britain, the party went from the monastery to Besançon and then north to Autun, stopping at the fortress of Cavalo. They continued north from Cavalo along the Roman road to the village of Chora, which had once served as the base of a Sarmatian military colony. (The toponymy indicates that the area continued to be influenced by these *laeti* throughout the Middle Ages.) Near Chora, a functionary of Theuderic's horse-breeding estates attacked Columbanus and tried unsuccessfully to kill him. Despite this and several other incidents, the group arrived at Auxerre where Ragamund seems to have reconsidered his plans; rather than continue north to Paris and the coast, he decided that the party should backtrack to Nevers where he could obtain boats to transport them to Nantes. These river craft (*scarfa*) carried not only the *custodes*, oarsmen, and prisoners, but tents and sufficient provisions for the several days' trip from Nevers north to Orléans.[11]

[10] *V. Columbani*, I, 19, 20. Fred., IV, 36, provides an abridged version of the story.

[11] *V. Columbani*, I, 20, 21, 22.

THE LAST OF THE RULING MEROVINGIANS

Upon reaching Nantes, Ragamund handed his prisoner over to Count Theudoald who was to arrange for Columbanus's deportation. The latter again escaped, however, and fled to the court of Chlotar II where he was given an armed escort for a journey to Italy. Going from Paris to Meaux and then to Pussy on the Marne, Columbanus left Chlotar's lands and entered the kingdom of Theudebert, who provided the missionary with guards (*comites e regio latere* and *custodes*) and manned boats for his travels on the Rhine.[12]

This account of the Columbanus affair provides additional evidence on the diverse nature of the Merovingian military. Like Theuderic I and Chilperic, Theuderic II utilized *milites* serving under *tribuni*. The direct relation of these *milites* with the Roman past is indicated in the sources, and therefore the inclination to assume that both Gregory and Jonas are employing obsolete imperial terms to describe a contemporary institution should be avoided. These authors use the word *milites* very sparingly and only when describing events about which they have reliable information. Gregory was at Tours when the *milites* there were mistreated by Count Leudast; Gregory's uncle was involved in the affair at Langres; and Jonas was a companion of Columbanus. Procopius, writing in the mid-sixth century, notes that even in his day the descendants of Roman soldiers once stationed in Gaul continued to perform the duties of their fathers.[13] The Merovingian monarchs regarded these descendants of imperial *milites* and imperial *laeti* within the framework of the personality of the law as quasi-national groups analogous in status to the *Romani*. The *milites* and the *laeti* were treated in the Salian law in this same manner as were their wives (*milituniae* and *laetae*) and daughters of marriageable age (*puellae laetae* and *puellae milituniae*).[14]

[12] *Ibid.*, I, 23, 24, 25, 26, 27.
[13] Gregory, *V.P.*, VII, 4; Gregory, *Hist.*, V, 48; and Procopius, *H.W.*, V, xii, 16ff.
[14] *Cap. Lex Sal. add.*, C, 4: "De puellas militu[n]ias vel litas haec lex medietate servetur." CIV, 9: "Aut Romanum ingenuum vel tributarium aut militem, solidos culpabilis iudicetur." See also *Lex Sal.*, 41, 8–10, and Pardessus, I, 49, ch. 9.

The Merovingian interest in legislating for these people suggests they were more important and more numerous than the few narrative accounts involving them might indicate. The rationale behind the official legal concern with these groups was based upon their importance as functioning armed forces within the Merovingian military and upon their institutional position, first under the empire and later under the monarchy. The *laeti* were a *corpus publicum* of the empire and probably came under the direct control of the Merovingian monarchs in the same manner as did the fisc, also a *corpus publicum*.[15] The similar treatment of the *milites* and the *laeti* in the Merovingian legislation implies that the former were also acquired by the monarchs. This would perhaps tend to explain the hostility at Tours between a count who sought to promote his own interests and *milites* who had a special tie to the king.

If the hypothesis above is correct — that the *milites* in Merovingian Gaul were descendants of imperial *milites* in title, vocation, and blood — then the *milites* serving under their *tribunus* at Besançon may perhaps be identified as the descendants of the *milites Batavi* who were stationed in that city during the fifth century.[16] Procopius remarks that in his day (about 550) some Roman units had survived in Gaul in the border areas.[17] (Besançon, approximately seventy-five miles west of the Rhine, would seem to fit that description.)

As has already been mentioned, Theuderic also used armed retainers from the court, *custodes*, and a magnate with his own followers against the intrigues of Columbanus. In addition, Theudebert provided *custodes* and Chlotar gave the exiled missionary an armed escort of *comites* from the court. The *custodes* referred to in these texts are treated similarly to those mentioned throughout the sixth century and seem to be some type of permanent armed group used by all the Merovingian kings. The *comites* at Chlotar's court do not seem to have been the kind of

[15] H. Pirenne, "Le fisc royal de Tournai," *Mélanges Ferdinand Lot* (Paris, 1925), p. 648, and Wallace-Hadrill, *Long-Haired Kings*, p. 153.
[16] *Notitia Dignitatum, oc.*, XXXVI, 5, n. 1: "Milites Batavi, Vesontione."
[17] Procopius, *H.W.*, V, xii, 16ff.

counts who administered cities, but rather were royal companions serving the king.[18] As further proof of the diverse nature of the Merovingian military organization, both Theuderic and Theudebert had organized water transport on at least the most important rivers in their territory, and Theuderic maintained stopping places at erstwhile imperial fortifications along the Roman roads in his kingdom.

In 610, the year following the Columbanus episode, Theudebert raided Alsace, which belonged to his brother. Soon after this, the brothers agreed to meet at the village of Seltz to settle their dispute. Theuderic arrived with two units — each of which Fredegar extravagantly asserts comprised 10,000 men — and Theudebert was accompanied by a large force of Austrasians with which he surrounded his brother's troops, thus ensuring for himself a favorable settlement. While the brothers were engaged at Seltz, Theubert's Alaman supporters raided Theuderic's territory around Avenches. The Counts Abbelin and Herpin, with other counts from the district, led their followers against the Alamans but were defeated and sustained severe losses.[19]

Though Fredegar exaggerates the size of Theuderic's force at Seltz, it was probably impressive to elicit such a reaction; and the Austrasian force which surrounded it must have been huge indeed. The term used to describe Theudebert's army — *magnus exercitus Austrasiorum* — might even suggest a special levy of some kind. Theuderic's troops, by contrast, are called *escaritos* and this is the only appearance of the term in medieval literature. *Escaritos* seems to have been replaced by the word *scarii* (the members of a *scara*).[20] These *scarii*, which were picked or special troops, are mentioned in the sources throughout the later Merovingian era. The *escaritos* commanded by Theuderic in 610 may be identified as a part of the *scara Burgundiae* which in turn may have been a part or all of the standing army of Burgundy discussed in the previous chapter. Theuderic's force which defended

[18] See the bibliography cited in ch. III, n. 60, above.
[19] Fred., IV, 37.
[20] J. F. Niemeyer, *Mediae Latinitatis Lexicon Minus* (Leiden, 1963), pp. 943–944. Cf. J. F. VerBruggen, "L'Armée et la strategie de Charlemagne," *Karl der Grosse* (Dusseldorf, 1965), I, 421–422.

the *pagus* of Avenches is said to have included many counts (*comites*), which implies that the term is being used here not in the formal sense of administrative and military leader of a *civitas* or *pagus*, but rather in the less technical sense of companion — similar perhaps to the *comites* who served at the court of Chlotar II.

In May of 612 Theudric assembled an army from all parts of his kingdom at Langres, a long-established Merovingian military base. Marching north from Langres through Andelot, he took the fortress of Naix and the fortified city of Toul — successes which should not be overlooked as evidence of his troops' capabilities in this type of warfare. While Theuderic traveled north through Andelot, Theudebert moved south with the forces of Austrasia, and the brothers' armies did battle at Toul. Theudebert was soundly defeated and he retreated by way of Metz and the Vosges to Cologne. Theuderic led his army through the Ardennes to Zulpich. Meanwhile, Theudebert, having been failed by the armies of Austrasia like his grandfather Sigibert I almost two generations earlier, summoned the tribes living beyond the Rhine. With Saxons, Thuringians, and other trans-Rhenish warriors under his command, Theudebert met Theuderic's forces at Zulpich. The carnage was so great that the chronicler Fredegar contends "men had nowhere to fall." Theudebert's forces were once again defeated; the king attempted to escape, but he was betrayed by his supporters and taken into custody by Berthar, a magnate who had pursued him in his flight.[21]

The mass scale of the battles at Toul and Zulpich has few if any parallels in Merovingian history. Theuderic called out men from all his lands, probably including the many local levies from his cities in Aquitaine and Neustria. At Toul Theudebert commanded only a force from Austrasia (*exercitus Austrasiorum*) which was apparently smaller and less strong than the one he called out in 610 (*magnus exercitus Austrasiorum*). Both these

[21] Fred., IV, 38: "Anno XVII regni sui Lingonas de universas regni sui provincias mense Madio exercitus adunatur, dirigensque per Andelaum, Nasio castra ceptum, Tollo civitate perrexit et cepit. Ibique Theudebertus cum Austrasiorum exercitum obviam pergens, Tollensem campaniam confligunt certamine." *V. Columbani*, I, 28, and cf. *L.H.F.*, ch. 38.

armies would seem to exclude Theudebert's local levies from Aquitaine and Neustria, as well as the territorial levy of Champagne. In any event, no details are known about the battle of Toul except that Theuderic was victorious. Not much has been recorded about the battle of Zulpich either, aside from the accounts of the great carnage. If Fredegar is not unduly exaggerating when he says the dead stood in their ranks unable to fall because there was no room, then it does not seem unreasonable to conclude that significant numbers on both sides were fighting on foot. This is a plausible assumption in light of the nature of the forces involved. Theudebert probably commanded what remained of the *exercitus Austrasiorum* which had been defeated at Toul, but his primary support came from the trans-Rhenish peoples, including Saxons who may well have provided the bulk of his infantry. Theuderic had called up a vast force from throughout his kingdom and there can be little doubt that many *pauperes* and *inferiores* had served at Zulpich. Some of Theuderic's forces, however, were mounted, such as Berthar's contingent which captured Theudebert after a hot pursuit. Berthar, incidentally, was given Theudebert's horse as a reward for his valuable service.

Shortly after his capture, Theudebert was put to death by his brother, who soon followed him to the grave, leaving his kingdom to his four young sons. Their great-grandmother Brunhild tried to serve as their regent, but Chlotar II, the only remaining adult Merovingian ruler, sought to take advantage of his cousins' youth by acquiring the allegiance of a group of their Austrasian and Burgundian magnates. Chlotar was able to occupy part of Austrasia because several Austrasian magnates and their followers defected from Brunhild. Brunhild's efforts to secure trans-Rhenish support were thwarted by the defection of Warnachar, mayor of the palace for Burgundy and Brunhild's envoy to the Thuringians. A number of the magnates, keeping their defection secret, accompanied Brunhild and her great-grandsons into the field against Chlotar. In the battle with the Neustrians some of Brunhild's troops simply deserted, while others captured the queen and her great-grandsons and handed them over to Chlotar who had them killed.[22]

With the death of Theudebert, Theuderic, and their heirs, Chlotar ruled all of Merovingian Gaul. Soon after achieving this position he issued the Edict of Paris by which he hoped to establish peace and order in his kingdom. Those magnates who had helped him gain control in Austrasia and Burgundy were rewarded with gifts and important offices.[23] Aware that the opposition of these powerful men could cause serious trouble, Chlotar and later his son Dagobert strove to avoid such difficulties by purchasing the loyalty of their *leudes* with offerings of offices, estates, and at times even church lands. Dagobert, for example, is alleged to have alienated church land so that he might ensure or perhaps secure the military support of certain magnates.[24] The memory of 605 when Theuderic II's magnates had refused to fight and killed the mayor of the palace, and of 612 when the defection of the magnates had brought about the death of Queen Brunhild and Theuderic's heirs may have motivated Dagobert's largesse when it came to maintaining the military support of the important men in Gaul. At any rate, Chlotar and Dagobert proved to be more adroit in dealing with their magnates than were Theudebert II and Theuderic II.

Chlotar and Dagobert were ruthless, however, in eliminating magnates who were troublemakers. Chlotar saw to it that Godinus — the son of Warnachar, the former mayor of the Burgundian palace — was killed along with a band of his followers. The task, which was first assigned to Duke Arnebert who failed, was finally accomplished by a magnate named Chramnulf and a *domesticus* by the name of Waldebert, when they and their followers cut down Godinus and his men at a villa near Chartres. The magnates Brodulf and Erminarius were killed because they plotted to overthrow Dagobert. Aighyna, a Saxon who later be-

[22] Fred., IV, 38, 39, 40, 41, 42.
[23] *Ibid.*, IV, 42; Wallace-Hadrill, *Long-Haired Kings*, pp. 214–216.
[24] *Mir. Martini Abbatis*, ch. 7: "Rex Dagobertus Francorum rei publicae princeps cum multis et variis bellorum eventibus premeretur, de coenobiis sanctorum multa abstulit, quae suis militibus est." See Boutaric, *Inst. milit.*, p. 68, and Bachrach, "Charles Martel," pp. 66–72.

came duke of Gascony, used his *pueri* to murder Erminarius, while the Dukes Amalgar and Arnebert, and Willebad, the patrician of Burgundy, did away with Brodulf. Arnebert also got rid of Boso of Étampes. Aighyna, Amalgar, and Arnebert all held the title *dux*, but were generally at the court and held no administrative position at the time they were assigned to kill those magnates whom Chlotar and Dagobert considered dangerous.[25]

From these examples of magnates who were eliminated it should not be concluded that Chlotar and Dagobert were victimized by rebellious *potentes*. On the contrary, both these monarchs enjoyed strong support from the important men of Merovingian Gaul. Though the transfer of power after the death of a ruler was usually a critical period, Dagobert succeeded his father with relatively little trouble by soliciting the aid of his magnates (*leudes*). This may call to mind the transition from the reign of Theuderic I to that of Theudebert I in 534, when the latter gained the support of his magnates (*leudes*) with gifts and was thus able to secure his throne in the face of his uncles' efforts to deprive him of it. Such comparatively easy transfers of power were rare during the Merovingian era, since the magnates often sought to take advantage of these situations by selling their support to opposition forces, or by creating an opposition themselves. Upon learning of Chlotar's death, Dagobert gathered his followers and their retainers *in exercito*, rode into Neustria, and secured the loyalty of the magnates there; shortly after, he repeated that process in Burgundy. Dagobert gave Aquitaine to his brother Charibert; Fredegar notes that this grant included the cities of Toulouse, Cahors, Agen, Périgueux, and Saintes, all of which had local levies with the possible exception of Cahors. Sometime after obtaining Aquitaine from Dagobert, Charibert brought Gascony under his control.[26]

Because Chlotar and Dagobert faced little internal opposition, both were able to spend the bulk of their military energy beyond the borders of Gaul. For example, in either 622 or 623 Dagobert led a large force across the Rhine to crush the Saxon rebellion

[25] Fred., IV, 54, 55, 58.
[26] *Ibid.*, IV, 56, 57.

against Merovingian domination. When Dagobert realized that his men were imperiled by the Saxon army, he sent word to his father for help. Upon receiving this request for aid, Chlotar roused his troops and moved from his camp in the Ardennes to the east. After traveling all night and part of the morning, Chlotar's force reached Dagobert's camp and pitched its tents. Angered by the remarks of the Saxon Duke Bertoald, Chlotar urged his horse into the river separating the Merovingian and Saxon camps and charged the enemy. Dagobert led his mounted followers across the river in support of his father and together they defeated the Saxons and brought about the death of Bertoald.[27]

When Dagobert had firmly secured his position within his own territory, he went to war against Samo, king of the Slavs, in 630. The Merovingian monarch organized a three-pronged attack against Samo's kingdom: the Lombards advanced from Italy, the Alamans from their Transjuran settlements, and the general levy of the Austrasian kingdom from the north of Gaul. Although the Lombards and the Alamans were successful, the Austrasians laid siege to the Slav fortress of Wogastisburg where they were decisively defeated in a three-day battle.[28]

The same year Dagobert arranged to send an army into Spain to support Sisenand, the Visigothic king, in his struggle for the throne; in return for this military aid he was to receive a 500-pound gold dish. Dagobert ordered the general levy of Burgundy and the local levy of Toulouse, which had come under his control after the death of his brother Charibert, to be called up. The levy of Toulouse, led by Venerandus and Abundantius, moved toward Saragossa but the Goths, seeing their peril, recognized Sisenand as king. Neither the general levy of Burgundy nor the local levy of Toulouse seems to have seen any action.[29]

[27] L.H.F., ch. 41.
[28] Fred., IV, 68.
[29] Ibid., IV, 73: ". . . Dagobertus . . . exercitum in ausilium Sisenandi de totum regnum Burgundiae bannire precepit." Cf. IV, 68: "Dagobertus . . . iubet de universum regnum Austrasiorum . . . movere exercitum. . . ." The former group seems to be a general levy from Burgundy and the latter a general levy from Austrasia. For the levy of Toulouse, IV, 73: "Abundancius et Venerandus cum exercito Tolosano tanto usque Cesaragustam civitatem cum Sisenando acesserunt. . . . Abundancius et Venerandus cum

In the following year Dagobert prepared to go against the Wends and summoned a force from Austrasia to take part in the battle. He had with him select detachments (*scara*) from Neustria and Burgundy, as well as numerous dukes and counts, presumably with their own personal followings. The campaign was canceled, however, when Dagobert arranged for the Saxons to be used against the Wends.[30]

Dagobert called up the general levy of Burgundy in 635 for the purpose of crushing a Gascon revolt. This force, under the command of Chadoind, a referendary, included ten dukes and Willebad, the Burgundian patrician, who probably commanded the Burgundian *scara*. Chadoind's men defeated the Gascons, who retreated into the mountains where they hid among the rocks and gorges while the Merovingian army devastated Gascony. The troops would have returned home with minimal losses had it not been for the negligence of Duke Arnebert, but he and his unit, in which were a number of important people (*seniores* and *nobiliores*), were massacred in the valley of the Soule. (It should be noted that none of the ten dukes who served under Chadoind in this campaign held administrative positions in specific territories. Aighyna was subsequently appointed duke of Gascony, but Arnebert, Amalgar, Chramnelen, and Barontus all served at Dagobert's court. The other five dukes are mentioned in no other Merovingian texts.)[31] In the same year as this Gascon uprising, Dagobert also threatened to send a Burgundian army into Brittany, but the mere threat brought the Bretons to terms.[32]

The heterogeneity of the Merovingian military persisted into the seventh century. That this diversity continued is proven by the number of different combinations of terms Fredegar uses to describe the Austrasian military: *magnus exercitus Austrasiorum, exercitus Austrasiorum, exercitus de Auster, exercitus de univer-*

---

exercito Tolosano munerebus onorati revertunt ad propries sedibus." See Gregory, *Hist.*, IX, 31, for an earlier mention of the levy of Toulouse. Cf. Thompson, *The Goths in Spain*, pp. 171–172.

[30] Fred., IV, 74.

[31] *Ibid.*, IV, 54, 58, for Arnebert; 58, 73, 90, for Amalgar; 67, for Barontus; 90, for Chramnelen; and 54, 55, for Aighyna.

[32] *Ibid.*, IV, 78.

sum regnum Austrasiorum, and *universi leudes in Auster in exercito.* The last of these phrases indicates an army of all the magnates of Austrasia, whereas *exercitus* and *magnus exercitus Austrasiorum* signify Austrasian forces of varying sizes. The *exercitus* from the *universum regnum Austrasiorum* is an army composed of inhabitants from all of Austrasia, and the *exercitus de Auster* seems to be territorial in nature. These Austrasian groups may be compared with the forces from Burgundy, which Fredegar calls an *exercitus de Burgundia* (a territorial levy), *exercitus de universum regnum Burgundiae,* and a *scara de elictis viris fortis de Burgundiae* (a group of select warriors which probably formed part of the standing army of Burgundy traditionally commanded by the patrician). The army of the entire Burgundian kingdom appears to have been some kind of general levy. There was also a *scara de elictis viris fortis de Neuster* which seems to have been some type of standing force. In the 570s and early 580s Chilperic commanded field forces which were not local city levies, general levies, *custodes,* or *milites;* for that matter they do not seem to have had any particular designation, but in view of their functions it is reasonable to conclude that they were a permanent military unit.[33] This force, so often seen serving under Chilperic, may well have been a Neustrian *scara* which went unlabeled by Gregory who was less apt than Fredegar to use germanisms.

The armies of Austrasia and Burgundy and the Neustrian *scara* were not the only fighting forces utilized by the Merovingian monarchs. The kings ruling in the northeastern parts of Gaul were able to obtain the military support of peoples from beyond the Rhine to compensate for the failures of the Austrasian armies during this period. This policy of enlisting the help of trans-Rhenish troops was followed by Theudebert I, Theudebald I, and Sigibert I during the sixth century and endured to the seventh. Theudebert's Alaman warriors from the eastern parts of what is now Switzerland were probably the descendants of those who had remained under Merovingian control after Clovis's victory of 506. Alamans, formed into a levy of some kind, fought

[33] Gregory, *Hist.,* IV, 23; V, 12, 24; VI, 31.

under the Alaman Dukes Leutharius and Buccelin in Theudebald I's campaign against Italy in 554, and continued to function well into the seventh century.

The local levies which were so prominent during the civil wars of Clovis's grandsons continued to be used by their successors, but in a much more limited manner. The reason for their limited value is that not only does a large amount of military action occur in the Austrasian and Burgundian kingdoms (which do not seem to have developed local levies at this time), but the extensive military action which took place beyond the borders of Gaul seems to have been beyond the competence of these these units. As has already been mentioned, the erstwhile imperial elements of the Merovingian military, especially the *milites*, continued to function, as did the *custodes*, whose basis of organization seems impossible to ascertain, the river fleets on the major waterways, and the fortified positions along major roads. Fredegar and the author of the *Liber Historiae Francorum* used the terms *comes* and *dux* much more loosely than did Gregory, and from their reports it may be suggested that many of the men who held such titles in this period functioned in much the same way as the untitled leaders of armed bands like Claudius who resided at the court of Clovis's grandson Guntram.[34]

The magnates and their bands of armed followers also provide another example of continuity in the Merovingian military. During this period of the last ruling Merovingians, the magnates still exerted as much influence on military and political affairs as they had in the past. Often their loyalty and support had to be purchased with expensive "gifts" as was the case when Chlotar II needed his magnates' aid to oppose the attack of Wintrio in 593. On occasion, however, the magnates were unwilling to lead their armed followings in the king's support, as in 605 when Theuderic's *leudes* refused to fight, or in 612 when the magnates who had promised their support to Theuderic II's sons and their regent, Brunhild, were bribed by Chlotar II and deserted the battle-

[34] See ch. III, n. 60, above.

field, thus causing the death of the queen and her great-grand-children. This was not altogether different from the desertion, slightly more than a century earlier, of Ragnachar's *leudes* which had cost him his kingdom and his life.

The monarchs also continued to support bands of personal armed followers: men who served them at the court wherever it might move. Several armed groups from Theuderic II's court saw action in the Columbanus affair, Chlotar II used his retainers to restrain his son Dagobert, and Theudebert II is said to have lost his life because of the faithlessness of his personal followers who allowed him to be captured by one of his brother's magnates.[35] These armed followings in attendance upon the king, including men called *duces* and *comites* in the sources, may be compared to the bands employed by the magnates, for the monarch after all was the most powerful magnate in the realm.

There seems to have been a certain continuity in the tactical maneuvers of the Merovingian military as well. Siege warfare, though less common than during the previous periods of Mero-vingian rule, was nevertheless used in the investment of Orléans and Wogastisburg. The relatively limited number of sieges was probably due to a change in the theaters of warfare from the more Romanized parts of Gaul with their fortresses and walled cities to the Austrasian hinterland and areas beyond the Rhine. Mass infantry tactics, though generally uncommon, appear once again when less Romanized barbarians from beyond the Rhine are introduced into Merovingian military affairs. Mounted forces, so conspicuous in Theuderic I's conquest of Thuringia in 531 and in the campaigns of Desiderius and Boso a generation or so later, were still evident in the operations undertaken during the reigns of the last ruling Merovingians.

The various types of levies, personal followings, and standing forces and the use of infantry, cavalry, siege operations, fortified positions, and organized transportation and communication in-dicate that the Merovingian military establishment and its tactics

[35] *Gesta Dagoberti*, ch. 8, and *V. Columbani*, I, 28.

were marked by both diversity and continuity during the period of the last ruling descendants of Clovis. The imperial and non-Frankish barbarian elements which lent support to the Merovingian leaders also illustrate this same continuity with the past as well as the debt the Merovingian military owed to groups in society other than the Franks.

CHAPTER V

The *Rois Fainéants* and the Mayors of the Palace: 638-751

NOT LONG after the death of King Dagobert in 638, his son Clovis II succeeded him as ruler of Neustria; Sigibert II, his elder son, had been king in Austrasia since 632. Because both monarchs were children, their reigns were supported and controlled by the magnates of their kingdoms. In Austrasia, Peppin of Landen, the mayor of the palace, and Bishop Chunibert of Cologne, who were the leaders among the magnates, assisted Sigibert in his political and military duties as king. According to Fredegar, the bishop and the mayor "skillfully and with suitable inducements drew the Austrasian magnates to their cause, and by treating them generously they gained their support and knew how to keep it."[1]

When Peppin died early in the year 639, a struggle erupted between Peppin's son Grimoald and Otto, the son of the *domesticus* Uro, for supremacy among the magnates. The weakness of the king's power in Austrasia was made manifest in 639 when Duke Radulf of Thuringia rebelled against royal control. Grimoald, on behalf of Sigibert (who was about eleven years old at that time), summoned the Austrasian magnates to put down the revolt. In addition to the personal followings of these *leudes*, a

---

[1] Fred., IV, 75, 79, 85: ". . . Pippinus cum Chuniberto . . . omnesque leudis Austrasiorum secum uterque prudenter et cum dulcedene adtradgentes, eos benigne gobernantes eorum amiciciam constringent semperque servandum."

general levy of the trans-Rhenish peoples living under Austrasian control and the local levies of the Saintois and of Mainz were also called to serve.[2] Grimoald, as Sigibert's commander, led the heterogeneous force across the Rhine and attacked a magnate named Fara, a supporter of Radulf and the son of the Agilolfing noble Chrodoald who had been killed on Dagobert's orders in 629. Fara and most of his followers were massacred; the few who survived were made slaves. Radulf, meanwhile, called up a levy from throughout Thuringia to oppose the Austrasian invasion and prepared for a siege in a stockade on a hill above the banks of the Unstrut in Thuringia. Sigibert's forces pitched their tents and laid siege to Radulf's position; however, Grimoald, who led the young king's army, became aware that he did not have the loyalty of all the magnates. Realizing that this lack of allegiance might endanger not only their position, but the life of the king as well, Grimoald and Duke Adalgisel made a great effort to guard Sigibert. The Austrasian monarch apparently did not have his own personal armed following to provide such protection.[3]

Despite the lack of solidarity in the army, Bobo, the duke of Auvergne and a loyal supporter of Grimoald, commanding some of Adalgisel's men, Count Innowales of the Saintois with the local levy of his district, and a large number of the remaining troops stormed the entrance to Radulf's fortifications. Radulf, knowing that several of Sigibert's dukes would not go against him, led his followers in a counterattack. Among those who did not support the king were the local levies of Mainz. Sigibert's forces suffered severe losses and had to obtain permission from Radulf to withdraw safely.[4]

[2] *Ibid.*, IV, 86, 87: ". . . Radulfus cux Toringiae vehementer contra Sigybertum revellandum disposuissit, iusso Sigyberti omnes leudis Austrasiorum in exercitum gradiendum banniti sunt. Sigybertus Renum cum exercito transiens gentes undeque de universis regni sui pagus ultra Renum cum ipsum adunati sunt." For the levies of the Saintois and of Mainz see n. 4 below.

[3] *Ibid.*

[4] *Ibid.*: "Bobo dux Arvernus cum parte exercitus Adalgyseli et Aenovales comex Sogiontinsis cum paginsebus suis et citeri exercitus manus plura contra Radulfum ad portam castri protenus pugnandum perrexerunt. . . . Macansinsis hoc prilio non fuerunt fedelis."

In the struggle for power in the first few years following Dagobert's death, the focus of the sources changes radically: more emphasis is placed on the activities of the mayors and the magnates than on those of the kings. In particular, Fredegar indicates how various magnates became mayors of the palace and acquired the support necessary to secure and defend their positions. Aega, the mayor of the palace for Neustria and an able man according to Fredegar, strengthened his position by alienating lands from the fisc and giving them to the magnates. After Aega's death in 642, Erchinoald succeeded to the mayorship of Neustria; in the following year, Erchinoald's friend and follower Flaochad became mayor of the palace in Burgundy and gained the support of the Burgundian magnates by promising in writing and by oath to protect them all in their honors and dignity and to give them his assistance. As noted above, Peppin made concessions and presented gifts to the Austrasian magnates to gain their loyalty. In short, Fredegar provides a glimpse of the process by which a magnate purchased the support of powerful men whose wealth and armed followers were vital to the exercise of power on a large scale. Grimoald's inability to unite effectively such men behind him was responsible in part for his defeat by Radulf in 639 and ultimately for his death in 656.[5]

In Burgundy Flaochad's position was endangered by the patrician Willebad, and in May of 643 Flaochad summoned a *placitum* at Chalons where Willebad was to be condemned. However, Willebad appeared with his followers, and discovering his peril, took Amalbert, Flaochad's brother, as hostage and escaped. In September of that year Flaochad returned from Paris to Burgundy with the child-king Clovis and a group of Neustrian

---

[5] *Ibid.*, IV, 80: "Facultatis pluremorum, quo iusso Dagoberti in regnum Burgundiae et Neptreco inlecte fuerant usurpate et fisci dicionebus contra modum iusticiae redacte, consilio Aegane omnibus restaurantur." That Aega, despite his avarice ("eo quod esset avariciae deditus"), should give lands of the fisc which he controlled to those from whom the late King Dagobert had taken them suggests that the mayor was obtaining some benefit from such transactions. See IV, 84, for Erchinoald, and 89: "Flaochadus cumtis ducibus de regnum Burgundiae seo et pontefecis per epistolas etiam et sacramentis firmavit, unicuique gradum honoris et dignetatum seo amiciciam perpetuo conservarit." See Ewig, "Teilreiche," pp. 114–120, and Bachrach, "Charles Martel," pp. 68–72.

magnates and their followers. Willebad, who realized he would
have to fight, called together a general levy from his patriciate,
his followers among the ecclesiastical and lay magnates, and what
may have been a part of the Burgundian standing army which
traditionally served under the patrician's command.[6]

Willebad advanced with his men to Autun where, after some
machinations, battle was joined with the combined forces of
Flaochad, Amalgar, Chramnelen, and Wandelbert. Erchinoald,
his Neustrian followers, and the Burgundian magnates who had
promised to support Flaochad remained spectators to the battle.
Berthar, a Transjuran Frank and count of the palace, was the first
to attack Willebad, but a Burgundian named Manaulf and his
followers charged Berthar and badly wounded him. However,
before the coup de grace could be delivered, Berthar's son
Chaubedo rode full tilt to his aid, knocking Manaulf to the
ground with his lance and killing his followers. In the ensuing
battle, Willebad and many of his men were slain. Those magnates who had not entered the battle plundered Willebad's camp
and seized a great deal of booty including a large number of
horses.[7]

In Neustria the struggle for power continued throughout the
second half of the seventh century. Erchinoald died in 657 and
was succeeded by Ebroin. After little more than a decade, Ebroin's support dwindled, and a group of Neustrian magnates
finally sent him into exile and chose as their leader Duke Wulfoald who was at that time the power behind Childeric II, the
Austrasian king and the son of Clovis II. Wulfoald, however,
alienated a faction of Neustrian magnates including Amalbert,
Ingobert, and Erchinoald's son Leudesius, who succeeded Wulfoald when he fled to Austrasia after a Frank named Bodilo
murdered King Childeric and his queen.[8] A short time later,
Ebroin, exiled at Luxeuil, called together his erstwhile supporters
(*socii*) and with a large following moved north against Leudesius

[6] Fred., IV, 89, 90: "Willibadus . . . colligens secum pluremam multi-
tudinem de patriciatus sui termenum, etiam et pontevecis seo nobelis et
fortis quos congrecare potuerat. . . ."

[7] *Ibid.*, IV, 90.

[8] Fred. con't., ch. 2.

and his puppet, King Theuderic IV, who were residing at a villa somewhere between Compiègne and Corbie. After a long hard ride from Luxeuil, Ebroin reached Pont-Saint Maxence on the Oise, found the unsuspecting guards (*custodes*) at the bridge asleep, and had them killed. Once Ebroin's men had crossed the Oise, word of their advance seems to have reached Leudesius who sent out a force to delay them. Meanwhile, Leudesius and his *socii* fled north with the king and the royal treasure. Ebroin destroyed those sent against him and pursued the royal party. At Basieux, some fifty miles from Pont-Saint Maxence, Leudesius abandoned the treasure so that his party might move more rapidly. But within another fifty miles Ebroin's men overtook and captured the royal treasure and the king. Leudesius and many of the magnates who supported him were put to death; others fled into exile south of the Loire.[9]

Early in the last quarter of the seventh century, a Merovingian king of strength and ability projected himself into this morass of royal puppets and contending magnates. Dagobert II, who had been banished to Ireland as a young man in the mid-650s, returned in the 670s with the aid of Bishop Wilfrith of York and with an armed following substantial enough to make credible his long hair and his claim to the throne. His efforts to restore royal power were opposed and, although he destroyed the strongholds of several magnates, he ultimately fell before the swords of an enemy faction. In this struggle for predominance Dagobert seems to have been not so much a king as just another magnate vying for supremacy — and not even the most powerful one as his ancestors had been.[10]

It should be noted that Dagobert, by having his own armed followers, seems to have been a rarity among the *rois fainéants*.

[9] *L.H.F.*, ch. 45; Fred. con't., ch. 2.
[10] *V. Wilfrithi*, ch. 28: "Et sic sanctus pontifex noster perfecit, suscipiens eum de Hibernia venientem, per arma ditatum et viribus sociorum elevatum magnifice ad suam regionem emisit." See also ch. 33, in which Dagobert is described as a "*dissipator urbium*" which Wallace-Hadrill, *Long-Haired Kings*, p. 238, n. 3, conjectures to mean that he destroyed city walls to keep them from being used as centers of resistance. For magnates in fortified cities cf. Fred. con't., ch. 4. Also in ch. 33 of the *V. Wilfrithi*, a bishop is described as leading a large warband.

For example, we have seen that as early as 639 Sigibert II had to rely on Duke Grimoald and Duke Adalgisel for his safety; Childeric II and his wife do not seem to have been protected by ubiquitous *pueri* like those who surrounded King Guntram. Yet oddly, among the formularies which were used in the chanceries of the *rois fainéants*, there are documents referring to the installation of *antrustiones* — armed followers including *pueri* who swore to serve the king in a military or paramilitary capacity in the *centenae* and probably at the palace as well. Since the kings during this period did not benefit from the assistance which these men were supposed to provide in return for support, then perhaps the mayors of the palace who controlled the royal fisc and chancery were served by these *fideles cum armis suis*.[11]

The struggle for power in Neustria had its counterpart in Austrasia. Grimoald was killed by a faction of magnates because he tried to place his own son on the throne instead of a Merovingian. After Grimoald's death, Wulfoald seems to have been the most successful magnate in Austrasia, and, as noted above, he even exercised considerable influence in Neustrian affairs for a time. At his death, and with "the disappearance of the kings [from Austrasia] Martin and Peppin, the younger son of the deceased Ansegisel, ruled over Austrasia." The Arnulfings once again established their supremacy as the premier magnates of Austrasia, and in fact ruled without a king.[12]

Martin and Peppin led a large force of Austrasians (*exercitum plurimum Austrasiorum commotum*) against the Neustrian mayor Ebroin but, in a battle at Bois du Fays near Rethel (*Ardennes*), Ebroin's men were victorious. Martin took refuge at Laon with his supporters (*sodales*) and his followers (*socii*), but they were massacred when they were tricked by Ebroin into

---

[11] Marculf, *form.*, I, 18: "Rectum est, ut qui nobis fidem pollicentur inlesam, nostro tueantur auxilio. Et qui illi fidelis, Deo propitio, noster veniens ibi in palatio nostro una cum arma sua in manu nostra trustem et fidelitatem nobis visus est coniurasse: propterea per presentem preceptum decernemus ac iobemus, ut dienceps memoratus ille inter numero antruscionorum conputetur. Et si quis fortasse eum interficere presumpserit, noverit se wiregildo suo soledos sexcentos esse culpabilem."

[12] Fred. con't., ch. 3; *L.H.F.*, ch. 46.

leaving. A Frank named Ermanfred and his *socii* then murdered Ebroin and fled to Austrasia where they were given protection by Peppin.[13]

After this campaign, the Neustrian magnates appointed Waratto mayor; he sought a policy of peace with the Austrasian mayor, but his son Ghislemar would not accept this policy. Ghislemar seized the fortified town of Namur, one of Peppin's strongholds, and killed many of Peppin's supporters who garrisoned the town.[14]

Shortly after this futile effort to establish peace, both Ghislemar and Waratto died, and Berchar, the latter's son-in-law, became mayor. Berchar, however, angered a number of Neustrian magnates, some of whom defected and joined Peppin in Austrasia. With the aid of these defectors and his own followers, Peppin was able to defeat Berchar, thus extending his authority over Neustria as well as Austrasia. St. Boniface, writing toward the middle of the eighth century, argues that church property had been taken over by secular magnates for at least sixty or seventy years and, although no specific text connects this spoliation of church lands with Peppin's rise to power, it is not unreasonable to suggest that he took over church lands and then gave them to his followers or would-be followers in order to secure and maintain their support.[15]

During the last decades of the seventh century Peppin gradually secured his position in Austrasia. He made his son Drogo duke of Champagne and his other son, Grimoald, mayor of the

[13] *L.H.F.*, ch. 46: ". . . hii duces in odium versi contra Ebroinum, exercitum plurimum Austrasiorum commotum, contra Theudericum regem et Ebroinum aciem dirigunt. Contra quos Theudericus et Ebroinus cum hoste occurrunt. . . ." Ewig, "Teilreiche," pp. 123–135.

[14] *L.H.F.*, ch. 47; Fred. con't., ch. 4.

[15] St. Boniface, *ep.*, 50: ". . . de aecclesiastica religione, quae iam longo tempore, id est non minus quam sexaginta vel septuaginta annos, calcata et dissipata fuit. . . ." The historical worth of this letter has been attacked, but the despoliation of church lands by monarchs and mayors before the accession of Charles Martel is indicated throughout the period. See the evidence presented by E. Lesne, *La Propriété ecclésiastique en France* (Paris, 1910), II, 2–6. See also Goffart, *Le Mans*, pp. 6ff, and the review of Goffart's work by Wallace-Hadrill, *Speculum*, XLIII (1968), 721–722. Bachrach, "Charles Martel," pp. 68–69. *L.H.F.*, ch. 48; Fred. con't., ch. 5.

palace to King Childebert. Peppin went to war against the Frisian Duke Radbod, defeated him, drove him from the fort at Duurstede, and returned home with a great deal of booty. Not only did Peppin increase his wealth by such expeditions, but he also strengthened his ability to keep the loyalty of his followers.[16]

Some details are known about one of Peppin's supporters, the *domesticus* Dodo. This man was well off economically and had in his service a band of private retainers (*pueri*) whom he provided with mail coats, helmets, shields, lances, swords, and bows and arrows. During the era of the *rois fainéants* it was the armed followers (*socii, pueri, sodales,* and *satellites*) of magnates like Dodo who formed the fighting forces in Austrasia and probably in Neustria. To be a successful mayor of the palace it was necessary to secure control of the forces these magnates commanded, and Peppin was most efficient at accomplishing this.[17]

Peppin's house suffered severe setbacks, however, when Drogo died of a fever and Grimoald was murdered. Grimoald's young son Theudoald was made mayor in his father's place. When Peppin died shortly thereafter, in 714, Theudoald was supported by his grandfather's *leudes,* men like Dodo, who provided much of the armed force to sustain him as mayor. But Theudoald proved to be a poor leader and the magnates soon transferred their allegiance to a certain Ragamfred and made him mayor. Ragamfred strengthened his position by allying with Radbod.[18]

As mayor of Austrasia, Ragamfred was primarily opposed by Peppin's bastard son Charles, who was later to obtain the sobriquet Martel. When Charles first began his struggle for power, he had only a small following and was almost destroyed. In 715 Ragamfred and Radbod led their warbands against Charles and

---

[16] *L.H.F.,* chs. 48, 49: Fred. con't., ch. 6.

[17] *V. Lamberti,* ch. 11: "In diebus illis erat Dodo domesticus iam dicti principes Pippeni, proprius con sanguinius eorum qui interfecti fuerant, et erant ei possessiones multae et in obsequio eius pueri multi." Also ch. 13: "Et erat multitudo copiosa virorum pugnatorum ad bellandum, et erat induit lurices et cassidis, clipeis et lanceis gladiisque precincti et sagittis cum pharetris."

[18] *L.H.F.,* chs. 48, 49; Fred. con't., chs. 6, 8: "Franci . . . contra Theudoaldum et leudis Pippino quondam atque Grimoaldo inierunt certamen. . . ." Also *L.H.F.,* ch. 51.

forced him to retreat. Shortly afterward, Ragamfred plundered the area around Cologne and obtained a large amount of treasure. While the mayor's force was returning home, Charles attacked it at Amblève near Malmédy and inflicted heavy losses. Although this seems to have been in the nature of a hit-and-run raid, its success probably raised the morale of Charles's followers.[19]

By March of 717, Charles had gained sufficient strength to attack Ragamfred who, having been defeated near Cambrai, fled south with his puppet king, Chilperic. Charles pursued them to Paris, but then abruptly reversed direction and sped to Cologne where he obtained his father's treasure and established Chlotar IV as king in Neustria.[20] There can be little doubt that by obtaining control of his father's treasure Charles's situation was benefited considerably. In the next year Charles defeated Radbod, who had routed him three years earlier. Apparently it had taken Charles all of three years, a victory over Ragamfred, and the acquisition of his father's treasure to secure the support necessary to defeat Radbod.[21]

Viewing Charles's rapid rise with alarm, Ragamfred sought the aid of Duke Eudo of Aquitaine. After the death of Dagobert I, Eudo's family had successfully established itself as the ruler of Aquitaine in much the same manner that other magnates had assumed control in Neustria, Austrasia, Thuringia, and Burgundy. Ragamfred obtained Eudo's aid with gifts and extravagant promises. Eudo led a levy of Gascons north against

[19] L.H.F., ch. 52: "Eo nempe tempore denuo exercitum movent, usque ipsum fluvium Mosam contra Carlum dirigunt; ex alia parte Frigiones cum Radbode duce consurgunt. Carlus quoque super ipsos Frigiones inruit, ibique maximum dispendium de sodalibus suis perpessus est, atque per fugam delapsus, abscessit." Fred. con't., ch. 9: "Contra quem praedictus vir Carlus cum exercitu suo consurgens certamen invicem inierunt. . . ." Note the use of *sodales* and *exercitus* as synonyms.

[20] L.H.F., ch. 53: "Eo itidem tempore predictus vir Carlus, exercitu commoto, iterum contra Chilpericum vel Ragamfredo consurgens." Fred. con't., ch. 10; Paul, *Hist.*, VI, 42: "Nam cum in custodia teneretur, divino nutu ereptus aufugit, ac primum contra Raginfridum cum paucis bis terque certamen iniit novissimeque eum aput Vinciacum magno certamine superavit."

[21] V. *Willibrodi*, ch. 13: "Qui multas gentes sceptris adiecit Francorum, inter quas etiam cum triumphi gloria Fresiam, devicto Rabbodo, paterno superaddidit imperio." See Wallace-Hadrill, *Fredegar*, p. 88, n. 2.

Charles, who, in turn, chased the Aquitanians south of the Loire. Charles then besieged Ragamfred at Angers, devastated the surrounding area, and returned home with a great quantity of booty.[22] During the next few years Charles defeated the Saxons and the Alamans, and subjugated the Bavarians. In 725 he led his followers in an amazing series of actions: first he crossed the Rhine and overwhelmed the Alamans, then he went south and subdued the Bavarians, and before the year was over he crossed the Loire and routed Duke Eudo once again.[23]

As Charles was consolidating his position with conquests and acquisitions of booty, Eudo was having to deal not only with him, but with frequent Muslim raids which devastated his lands. Eudo's supporters garrisoned the fortified cities and fortresses of Aquitaine, but in 721 the Arab leader al-Samh besieged and took Narbonne and then laid siege to Toulouse. Eudo, however, with a force of Aquitanian and Frankish followers — the latter perhaps descendants of the magnates exiled to Aquitaine by Ebroin several decades earlier — defeated al-Samh's army and drove it from Gaul. The Arab leader was slain, but his successor, 'Anbasa ibn Suhaim al-Kalbi, was more successful; he captured, or more probably besieged, Carcassonne and Nîmes. He raided as far north as Autun and perhaps even as far as Luxeuil. While this Arab force concentrated in Burgundy, another group, commanded by Abd al-Rahman, moved into Aquitaine and in the summer of 732 went against Bordeaux. At the confluence of the Dordogne and the Garonne, Eudo met Abd al-Rahman's army and was soundly defeated. As the duke of Aquitaine fled north to seek the aid of Charles, the Arabs also moved northward, sacking the Church of St. Hilary at Poitiers and then taking the road for Tours.[24]

[22] *L.H.F.*, ch. 53; Fred. con't., chs. 10, 11.
[23] Fred. con't., chs. 11, 12, 13.
[24] *Chron. Moissiac*, p. 290; Fred., con't., chs. 42, 43, 44. E. Lévi-Provençal, *Histoire de l'espagne musulmane* (Paris, 1950), I, 58; M. Baudot, "Localisation et datation de la première victoire remportée par Charles Martel contre les Musulmans," *Mémoires et documents publiées par la Société de l'Ecole des Chartes*, XII (1955), 93–105, is very probably mistaken in setting 733 as the date for this battle. Michel Rouche, "Les Aquitans

In October Charles met the Arab army somewhere between Poitiers and Tours and decisively defeated it. Though few details concerning the battle of Poitiers can be ascertained, it has received a great deal of attention, probably because it has symbolized for many the turning back of the Muslims and the saving of Christendom.[25] Only two texts — somewhat contradictory in nature — provide information of apparent historical value about the battle. According to the continuator of Isidore's chronicle, ". . . the people of the North seemed like a wall, enduring unmoveable, and like a firm glacial mass they remained together, cutting down the Arabs with their swords."[26]

Fredegar's continuator asserts that ". . . Charles boldly prepared his troops and aggressively charged the enemy. With Christ's help he overthrew their tents. He continued the battle slaughtering and destroying, and when their king Abd al-Rahman was killed, he destroyed them, crushing the army. He fought and conquered; victorious over his enemies he triumphed."[27]

The Isidorian continuator establishes a literary conceit by referring to the "people of the North" (*gentes septentrionales*) and by describing their formation metaphorically as a "firm glacial mass" (*zonis rigoris glacialiter*). Despite these affectations the author's main thrust seems to emphasize the stolidness of Charles's followers; *permaneo* (to endure, hold out, stay to the end) and *maneo* (to stay or remain) are the verbs used to charac-

ont-ils trahi avant la bataille de Poitiers?" *Le Moyen Age,* 74 (1968), 25–26, presents a very convincing argument based largely on the Arab sources for the traditional date of 732. See also Bachrach, "Charles Martel," pp. 72–73, and Donald Bullough, *"Europae Pater*: Charlemagne and His Achievement in the Light of Recent Scholarship," *EHR,* LXXV (1970), 84–89.

[25] Jean-Henri Roy and Jean Devoisse, *La Bataille de Poitiers* (Paris, 1966), 334–335, provide an extensive list of works on the battle of Poitiers.

[26] *Isidori continuatio Hispana,* chs. 104–105, pp. 361–362: ". . . gentes septentrionales in hicto oculi ut paries inmobiles permanentes sicut et zona rigoris glacialiter manent adstricti, Arabes gladio enecant." This chronicler also has been called Isidorus Pacensis and the Anonymous of Cordoba.

[27] Fred. con't., ch. 13: "Contra quos Carlus princeps audacter aciem instruit, super eosque belligerator inruit. Christo auxiliante tentoria eorum subvertit, ad proelium stragem conterendam accurrit interfectoque rege eorum Abdirama prostravit, exercitum proterens, dimicavit atque devicit; sicque victor de hostibus triumphavit."

terize the Northerners' posture in face of the enemy. By dwelling on this theme of stolidness, especially in his use of verbs, and by avoiding the use of *sto* (to stand) the Isidorian chronicler suggests a comparison with those who fled instead of enduring or persevering in the face of the enemy. Throughout the Merovingian era both the Visigoths and the Gascons had a well-established reputation for turning their back and fleeing in face of the enemy rather than remaining bravely on the field of battle. It seems reasonable that behind his metaphors the Isidorian chronicler is commenting not upon the Northerners' tactics, but upon their bravery and courage.[28]

The problems caused by the ambiguity of the Isidorian's metaphorical style are probably of less consequence than those resulting from uncritical acceptance of his remarks. In short, Isidore's continuator is not reliable. He presents legend as fact and makes obvious errors indicating his lack of familiarity with affairs north of the Loire, as well as with affairs in Aquitaine. For example, he calls Eudo "duke of the Franks" (*dux Francorum nomine Eudo*), when in truth he held no such title. The chronicler also refers to Charles's followers as *Europenses*. The use of this term supports those who contend that the work was not a late eighth-century composition but a creation of the later Middle Ages. If indeed the entire chronicle is not later medieval then it was surely interpolated during the later Middle Ages.[29]

[28] For the Visigoths, Gregory, *Hist.*, II, 37. For the Gascons, Fred., IV, 78: "Wascones deinter moncium rupes aegressi, ad bellum properant. Cumque priliare cepissint, ut eorum mus est terga vertentes. . . ." See also Fred. con't., chs. 44; 47: ". . . set statim solito more omnes Wascones terga vertunt. . . ." See Bachrach, "Feigned Retreat," pp. 265–266.

[29] Levison, *Deutschlands Geschichtsquellen*, I, 91, indicates the unreliability of this text as does F. Codera, "Manusa y el duque Eudon," *Estudios críticos de historia árabe-española* (Saragossa, 1903), 140–169, in vol. VII of the *Colección de los estudios árabes*. Lévi-Provençal, *Hist. de l'esp. mus.*, I, 60–61, is less critical of the Isidorian continuator than is Codera. The entire text, however, is in need of detailed restudy. Concerning "Europenses," D. Hay, *Europe: The Emergence of an Idea* (Edinburgh, 1957), p. 25, accepts the eighth-century date, post-754, for the use of the term. But throughout his work, Hay adduces no other examples of the term being used in either the early or the high Middle Ages. The term does not take hold until the late Middle Ages, if indeed that early. For a long time scholars considered the text of the Isidorian continuator to be a sixteenth-

In contrast to the continuator of Isidore's chronicle, the continuator of Fredegar's chronicle seems to be the most trustworthy source for the career of Charles Martel. Count Childebrand, Charles's half-brother, and probably a participant in the battle of Poitiers, sponsored and oversaw the writing of the section concerning this particular battle.[30] It would seem unlikely that the count would have permitted Fredegar's continuator to describe the battle inaccurately — that is, if Charles's followers had stood in a phalanx the count would not have allowed the chronicler to write that they charged the enemy or vice versa. Thus it seems reasonable to accept this version of the story.

Throughout the rest of his life, Charles campaigned vigorously. The year after his victory at Poitiers he invaded Burgundy with his magnates and their followers, and subjugated it to his authority. He then gave his *leudes* lands in the Lyonnais so that they could maintain his interests in Burgundy. At about the same time or perhaps a little earlier, Charles gained control of the Orleanais, confiscated the holdings of his enemies in the area, and granted some of this wealth to his *satellites*.[31]

In 734 Charles led a naval expedition against the Frisians who had rebelled against him. His fleet penetrated between the islands of Westergo and Ostergo, he encamped on the banks of the Boorn, defeated the Frisians, killed their leader Bubo, and returned to *Francia* with an abundance of spoils.[32] While Charles was in Frisia, Eudo died. Charles therefore gathered the magnates of his kingdom together with their followers; they crossed the Loire and traveled to Bordeaux and then to Blaye. He pro-

---

century forgery (Levison, p. 91); Roy and Devoisse, *Poitiers*, pp. 293–294, seem to accept a late date: "Extrait de l'anonyme de Cordoue (vers 1376–1437)." The *Chron. Moissiac*, p. 290, calls Eudo "princeps Aquitaniae."

[30] Fred. con't., ch. 34: "Usque nunc inluster vir Childebrandus comes avunculus praedicto rege Pippino hanc historiam vel gesta Francorum diligentissime scribere procuravit." This was written about 752 and antedates the earliest possible date for the Isidorian continuator by at least two years. Some scholars argue for two battles or encounters in the Poitiers campaign. It is of course possible but unlikely that Isidore's continuator described one engagement and Fredegar's continuator another.

[31] Fred. con't., ch. 14. Bachrach, "Charles Martel," pp. 66–68. Bullough, "Europae Pater," pp. 84–89. Cf. White, *Med. Tech.*, p. 12.

[32] Fred. con't., ch. 17.

ceeded to occupy Eudo's lands, including the cities and fortresses of southwestern Gaul.[33] During the next three years Charles subdued the Burgundian magnates of the Lyonnais once again and placed the area as far south as Marseilles under the leadership of his own counts. This southern expansion brought Charles into contact with Maurontus and his supporters (*socii*) who had taken the fortified city of Avignon and devastated the surrounding area. Charles sent Childebrand and several counts and dukes with their followers against Maurontus. They laid siege to Avignon, and when Charles arrived, the besiegers made their assault; battering rams were brought into action and rope ladders were used to scale the walls. The city was taken and its garrison was destroyed. Charles then moved his men against Narbonne; siege was laid to the city and engines for its destruction were brought into place. Charles did not complete the siege of Narbonne because he was distracted by the Arabs, led by Iussef ibn Abd ar Rahman, who were encamped not far from Narbonne. Charles turned his attention to them and his forces besieged their camp. When the Arab governor Ukba ibn al-Hadjdjadj learned of Charles's activity in the south, he advanced against him with a large army. On the swampy banks of the Berre in the valley of Corbières the Arabs were defeated; Charles's followers, taking to boats, cut down those survivors who tried to escape across the river. After obtaining a rich booty from the conquered Arabs, Charles devastated the area around Nîmes, Agde, and Beziers. While Charles was fighting the Arabs, the Saxons revolted; he therefore hurried north and decisively crushed them. In 737 Charles also sent Childebrand with many dukes and counts into Provence. The Avignon area was once again subjugated and Maurontus, who seems to have returned to the city at the time when Charles was in the west, fled to an island fortress in the Mediterranean.[34]

In the span of a quarter century Charles Martel accomplished a feat not unlike that of Clovis more than two centuries earlier.

[33] *Ibid.*, ch. 15; cf. Fred., IV, 56.
[34] Fred. con't., chs. 18, 19, 20, 21; *Chron. Moissiac*, p. 292. See Lévi-Provençal, *Hist. de l'esp. mus.*, I, 63.

Beginning with a small personal following, Charles increased his power by winning military victories and acquiring wealth in land and treasure which he used to buy the support of the magnates and their armed retainers.

In approximately 740 Charles divided control of the lands under his sway between his sons Carloman and Peppin. Carloman was given Austrasia, Swabia, and Thuringia, and Peppin received Burgundy, Neustria, and Provence. The same year Peppin and his uncle Childebrand with a following of magnates and their followers entered Burgundy and once again asserted Carolingian control.[35]

When Charles died in October 741, a crisis arose comparable to those which had accompanied the deaths of Merovingian kings a century or two earlier. His daughter Childtrudis married the Bavarian Duke Odilo, her brothers' enemy. Duke Chunoald of Aquitaine, the late Eudo's son, revolted against Carloman and Peppin, as did the Alamans, and shortly after this Odilo rose in rebellion.[36] Peppin and Carloman moved their forces (*exercitus*) at once against Chunoald. After defeating a levy of *Romani* which opposed them at Orléans, the brothers moved south to Bourges, burning the surrounding area. They continued their pursuit of Chunoald, devastating the land through which they traveled. They successfully besieged the enemy fortress of Loches, captured the garrison (*custodes*) there, and breached the walls making them indefensible. Carloman and Peppin then divided the booty they had taken and recrossed the Loire with many prisoners. In the autumn of the same year, soon after returning from Aquitaine, the brothers set out with their men (*exercitus*) again — this time against the Alamans. They crossed the Rhine and moved south, camping on the banks of the Danube. When the Alamans were confronted by Peppin and Carloman's army, they capitulated; recognizing their subject status, they gave gifts and hostages to the Carolingian mayors.[37]

[35] Fred. con't., chs. 23, 24: ". . . Pippinus dux, commoto exercito, cum . . . Childebrando duce et multitudine primatum et agminum satellitum plurimorum Burgundia dirigunt. . . ."
[36] *Ibid.*, chs. 25, 26.
[37] *Ibid.*, ch. 25.

Rois Fainéants AND MAYORS OF THE PALACE

In the winter of 743 the brothers found it necessary to move against Odilo. To supplement their Frankish followers, the brothers called up a general levy to deal with the Bavarians. For a fortnight the forces of the mayors and the Bavarian duke faced each other on the banks of the Lech at Apfeldorf near Epfach. Finally one night the Carolingian army made its way through the marshy terrain surrounding Odilo's position and advanced from a direction where they were least expected since there was no causeway. The attack succeeded and Odilo barely escaped with a small group of his men. Both sides, however, suffered severe losses.[38]

Fredegar's continuator indicates that the brothers were compelled to call up a general levy for the Bavarian campaign. This was the first time in more than a century that such a force had been called up in Austrasia, and probably in Neustria as well. To enhance their position, and perhaps to legitimize their summoning such a force, the Carolingian rulers filled the vacant kingship with the Merovingian Childeric III. The brothers' previous successes in Aquitaine and against the Alamans may also have strengthened their position. Nevertheless, the Bavarian revolt seems to have been critical and the pious Carloman who had been working for church reform found it essential to retain secularized church lands in 743. He justified his action on the grounds that he required the revenue to support his military campaigns in those days when warfare was raging or threatening on all sides.[39]

The year following the defeat of Odilo, Carloman's forces (*exercitus*) invaded the Saxon borderland and the inhabitants submitted without a fight. At the same time the Alaman Duke Theudebald revolted. Peppin, commanding a force of his picked men ("cum virtute exercitus sui"), journeyed into the Swabian

[38] *Ibid.*, ch. 26: "Conpulsi sunt generalem cum Francis in Bagoaria admoveri exercito venientesque super fluvium qui dicitur Lech. . . ."

[39] *Ibid.*, MGH *Cap.*, I, no. 11, 2: "propter inmentia bella et persecutiones ceterarum gentium quae in circuitu nostro sunt . . . in adiutorum exercitus nostri." The Pope accepted Carloman's actions and recognized that the mayor's military activities also benefited the church. (*MGH epist.*, iii, no. 324.)

107

Alps, drove Theudebald from his rocky retreat, and once more subjected the duchy. The next year the brothers invaded Gascony; the inhabitants, after first provoking the mayors, succumbed without a battle. The Alamans, however, again rebelled and Carloman's army (*exercitus*) crushed them and he executed many.[40]

In 747 Carloman retired to a monastery and Peppin ruled alone. The Saxons rebelled against their new ruler, breaking the oath they had sworn earlier to Carloman. Peppin's followers (*exercitus*), with the help of the Wends and the Frisians, invaded Saxon territory; the Saxons submitted without a fight and promised to pay an annual tribute of 500 cows. The Bavarians revolted in 749 and Peppin moved against them with a large force. The rebels fled across the Inn and Peppin established his camp on the banks of the river, preparing to attack the enemy from the river craft which he ordered to be made ready for that purpose. Seeing the imminence of the peril presented by Peppin's naval preparations, the Bavarians decided to yield without a fight.[41]

Throughout the next two years Peppin ruled in peace and his Merovingian puppet, Childeric III, reigned from his oxcart. First with Carloman, and later alone, Peppin had subjugated the former Merovingian kingdoms (except Aquitaine) to his control. In 751 this Carolingian mayor, the true ruler of Gaul, became *Rex Francorum*, replacing the Merovingian who merely reigned. Thus the Merovingian dynasty came to an end and with it the epoch of the mayors and the *rois fainéants*.[42]

The military in this era (638–751), as described in the numerous campaigns treated above, cannot be characterized with a simple generalization. In 638 Dagobert had left his sons a very complex military organization. The Roman heritage was preserved in the *milites*, fortress garrisons, and *centenae*, and to some degree in naval organization on the major rivers, and in defensive organization on the old Roman road system. The

[40] Fred. con't., chs. 27, 28, 29.
[41] *Ibid.*, chs. 30, 31, 32.
[42] *Ibid.*, ch. 33: ". . . commoto exercito cum magno agmine apparatu. . . ."

other important groups functioning during the era of the last ruling Merovingians (593–638) were local levies, regional levies, general levies, standing forces (*scara*), and the personal followings of the magnates and the kings.

For a short while after Dagobert's death no great changes seem to have taken place in the military of Merovingian Gaul, with the exception that authority passed from the monarch to the mayors of the palace and other important magnates. In 639 a regional levy of Austrasians from beyond the Rhine, the local levies of the Saintois and Mainz (probably first organized by Dagobert I or his father), and the followings of the Austrasian magnates were called to service. These forces were used against the rebellious Duke Radulf of Thuringia who summoned his regional levy and his supporters among the magnates with their followers. In Burgundy a few years later, the patrician Willebad called up a general levy of his patriciate, the remains of the Burgundian standing army which was traditionally led by the patrician, and the magnates who supported him, both lay and ecclesiastical, with their followers. This force was opposed by the mayors of Neustria and Burgundy with their personal retainers and those of the magnates who supported them.

The Willebad affair is only one illustration of the importance of the personal retainers during this period. For it can be said that from the 640s on the main forces operating under the command of the mayors and other magnates were the personal armed followings. Ebroin regained his place as mayor of the palace in Neustria with the help of his followers (*socii*). He was later killed by a Frankish magnate named Ermanfred and his *socii*. King Dagobert II made an effort to reestablish royal power with the help of a personal armed following of *socii* supplied to him by Bishop Wilfrith. The *antrustiones* who once served the kings in the *centenae* and at the court (*cum armis suis*) were probably still recruited, but now used their arms to fight in the service of the mayors of the palace who controlled the fisc and provided for their support. On occasion some magnates would become powerful enough to organize a group of warbands. Thus Peppin II and Duke Martin gathered a large force of Austrasians composed of *sodales* and *socii* to attack Ebroin. Peppin also used loyal magnates with their followers, or perhaps his own personal retainers, to garrison strongholds under his control.

The forces led by Charles Martel and Peppin III are described with some consistency by Fredegar's continuator. On four occasions Charles's army is simply called an *exercitus*.[43] One of these forces which the continuator calls an *exercitus* is described by the author of the *Liber Historiae Francorum,* upon whom the former relies, as being formed of Charles's *sodales*.[44] At one point Fredegar's continuator depicts Charles's army as an *agmen multitudo* and at another time as a *hostis Francorum*.[45]

Fredegar's continuator describes eight of the forces led by the mayors Carloman and Peppin III before the latter became king. All but one of these are described simply as *exercitus*.[46] The remaining body is called an *exercitus generalis cum Francis* or a general army including Franks.[47] Thus eleven of the fourteen forces led by the mayors during the last thirty-five years of the Merovingian era concerning which there is a clear description are denoted by the term *exercitus.* Both Fredegar and his continuator consistently use the term *exercitus* to mean a personal armed following during the period of the last two Carolingian mayors. When Fredegar's continuator wants to indicate some other kind of force (such as a general levy), he uses a term like *exercitus generalis.* Some additional light on the nature of the term *exercitus* as utilized by Fredegar's continuator may be obtained from a description of Peppin's forces in 740: "Peppinus . . . commoto exercito, cum avunculo suo Childebrando duce et multitudine primatem et agminum satellitum plurimorum. . . . "[48]

The personal armed followings of the magnates seem to have dominated the military in Austrasia, and this was probably the case in Neustria and perhaps also in Burgundy. In Aquitaine, the most Romanized part of Gaul, a more complex military structure

---

[43] *Ibid.,* chs. 9, 10, 13, 18.
[44] *L.H.F.,* 52.
[45] Fred. con't., chs. 12, 19.
[46] *Ibid.,* chs. 24, 25, 27, 29, 31, 32.
[47] *Ibid.,* ch. 26.
[48] *Ibid.,* ch. 24.

survived: a general levy of Gascons (*hostis Vascanorum*) functioned, as did local levies such as the *Romani* at Orléans. The fortified cities and many fortresses of Aquitaine were provided with
garrisons.[49]

Though there seems to have been some simplification in military organization during the era of the mayors, tactics remained
quite similar to those of earlier times. Siege operations, so common throughout the Merovingian era, continued, especially in
the more Romanized parts of Gaul. In 737 when Charles Martel
invaded southern Gaul he laid siege to Avignon, attacked the
walls with battering rams, used rope ladders to scale the heights,
and took the fortress. Dagobert II attacked fortified positions
as did Ghislemar who took the fortress at Namur belonging to
Peppin II, who, in turn, besieged the fortified city of Duurstede.
Naval operations also remained a part of Merovingian military
capability. Charles led a sea invasion of the Frisian islands in 734,
and in 737 his forces used river craft to cut off a Muslim retreat
on the river Berre. Peppin prepared naval craft to go against the
Bavarians in 749. Mounted operations also do not seem to have
been neglected by the mayors during this last period of Merovingian history. Ebroin's pursuit of Leudesius and Theuderic IV was
surely carried out on horseback. Charles Martel's hit-and-run
raids in 715, his campaign in 717, and his threefold campaign of
725 in which he fought the Alamans across the Rhine, subdued
the Bavarians in southern Germany, and crossed the Loire to raid
in Aquitaine were most likely carried out at least in part by
mounted forces. Actual evidence for cavalry charges is limited.
Charles's forces which fought on the swampy banks of the Berre
would have had little chance to fight on horseback; Peppin's
troops who in 743 picked their way through the marshy terrain
at Apfeldorf where there was no causeway could not possibly
have been mounted; and it is unlikely that Peppin's followers who
drove the Alaman Duke Theudebald from the Swabian Alps kept
to their horses. It is more difficult to find clear-cut instances of
mounted activity from 639 to 751 than it was in earlier periods of

[49] *Ibid.,* chs. 15, 20, 25, 46.

Merovingian history. Chaubedo's attack in 643 seems to have been more a personal effort than a mass charge, and not comparable to Theuderic I's charge across the Thuringian plains in 531 or Landri's at Soissons in 593 or Dagobert's against the Saxons in 623. Under the mayors of the palace there seem to have been no mounted shock attacks after the battle of Poitiers; though at the battle itself Charles Martel's followers who charged the Muslims, overran their tents, and pursued them hotly may well have done so on horseback and not on foot.[50]

Thus, although the Merovingian kings gradually lost control of Gaul to the mayors and the magnates, their military organization, which had become more diverse through the centuries, but had retained much of the Roman past, continued to play a significant and influential role in this last century of Merovingian history.

[50] Bachrach, "Charles Martel," pp. 53–57.

CHAPTER VI

Conclusion

ALTHOUGH previous studies dealing with Merovingian military organization have been limited to a small selection of the available evidence, the methods and conclusions of the more influential scholarly works are worth discussing if only to indicate how they might have benefited from a use of the entire corpus of evidence.

In his *Institutions militaires de la France* which appeared in 1863, Edgard Boutaric devoted some nineteen pages to the military of "la première race."[1] He argued that the Franks as an ethnic group in the Merovingian kingdoms were only a minority of the population and had to rely heavily upon their Gallo-Roman subjects for both the conquest and the defense of Gaul.[2] Nevertheless, when discussing the armament and organization of the Merovingian armies, Boutaric seems to ignore his earlier remarks and the evidence on which they are based and allows the Byzantine historian Agathias's characterization of the Franks as an ethnic group to serve as a description of the rank and file of the Merovingian armies.[3] Boutaric does argue, however, that the mounted bodyguards of the kings and the armed followers of

---

[1] Paris, 1863, pp. 50–69.
[2] Boutaric, *Inst. milit.*, pp. 50–54. Fustel de Coulanges, *Hist. des inst.*, IV, 293ff, generally agrees with this conclusion.
[3] Boutaric, *Inst. milit.*, pp. 64–65.

the magnates formed a class of professional soldiers and played an important role in the Merovingian military.[4] He further maintains that imperial influence was felt especially in the organization of siege warfare.[5] Perhaps the most crucial weaknesses of Boutaric's work are the inadequate length of his study, which does not allow full exploitation of the sources, and his neglect of the military during the last century of Merovingian history.

Boutaric's balanced though limited account of the Merovingian military has won few adherents among the most influential historians in the field. From the many articles, essays, and chapters of general works which have appeared since 1863, an image of the Merovingian military emerges of poorly armed and ill-disciplined levies of infantrymen performing military service in response to a primal Teutonic duty owed by all freemen. Roman military institutions are generally regarded as having ceased to exist, and the numerically preponderant and tactically decisive elements of the Merovingian military from 481 until at least 732 are the farmer-soldiers of the *pagi* fighting under their counts. With the general acceptance of this view, scholars have devoted their efforts to ascertaining when and under what circumstances these levies of Frankish footmen, supported on occasion by Gallo-Romans, were replaced by heavily armed knights who, serving as feudal vassals, are alleged to have dominated the battlefields of Europe during the Middle Ages.[6]

Heinrich Brunner's 1887 article, "Der Reiterdienst und die Anfänge des Lehnwesens," embodies what is today the dominant picture of the Merovingian military.[7] Relying heavily upon the writings of Procopius and Agathias, Brunner unequivocally

---

[4] *Ibid.*, pp. 64–67. Fustel de Coulanges, *Hist. des inst.*, IV, 289, argues the opposite: "L'armée composée de vrais soldats c'est désorganisée et disparu."

[5] Boutaric, *Inst. milit.*, p. 66.

[6] Claudio Sánchez-Albornoz, *En torno a las Orígenes del Feudalismo* (Mendoza, 1942), III, 1–27, and Lynn T. White, Jr., *Medieval Technology and Social Change* (Oxford, 1962), pp. 5, 6, 7, 137, and 138.

[7] *ZRG*, VIII, 1–38, reprinted in Brunner, *Forschungen zur Geschichte des deutschen und französischen Rechts* (Stuttgart, 1894), pp. 39–74. All citations here are to the former. See also Brunner, *Deutsche Rechtsgeschichte*, 2nd ed. (Munich, 1928), II, 269ff. Cf. Georg Waitz, *Deutsche Verfassungsgeschichte* (Berlin, 1882), II, *passim*.

CONCLUSION

equates their descriptions of the tribal military customs of the
Franks as an ethnic group with the military customs of the Merovingian armies.[8] Brunner drew his account of a horde of half-naked
infantrymen armed with axes and barbed spears who performed
military service because they were freemen from these two Byzantine writers, neither of whom had ever seen a Merovingian
army, much less a purely Frankish fighting force. Brunner cites
as supporting evidence for his view an Anglo-Saxon poem which
has been dated variously from the eighth to the tenth century.
According to Brunner, this poem provides accurate evidence for
an event that took place in Gaul about 515. In developing his
argument Brunner neglects Gregory of Tours's account of this
episode in 515 which does not support the thrust of the considerably later English text. To round out his study of Merovingian
military tactics, Brunner cites a passage from Gregory of Tours
describing Clovis splitting open the head of a warrior with an
ax. From these four accounts — two Byzantine, one Anglo-Saxon,
and one Merovingian — none of which deals with the period
after 560, Brunner concludes that Merovingian military tactics
and armament from 481 to 732 were synonymous with the tribal
practices of the Franks in all significant aspects. The 732 date
for the terminus of this form of organization and tactics is provided for Brunner by the description of the battle of Poitiers
given by the continuator of Isidore's chronicle in which Charles
Martel's armies are alleged to have fought on foot. To help support his argument that a great change was wrought in the military after this battle, Brunner cites a provision of the Ripuarian
Frankish law which lists horses, arms, and armor in a manner
which might lead to the conclusion that the national weapons of
the Franks had been changed not only in fact but also in law
during the eighth century.[9] Brunner apparently was unaware of

[8] Brunner, "Reiterdienst," pp. 2–3.
[9] *Ibid.*, pp. 3–4, and 13–16. *Lex Rib.*, 40, 11: "Equum . . . sanum pro
septem solid. tribuat. Spatam cum scoigilo pro septem solid. tribuat. . . .
Brunia bona pro duodecim solid. tribuat. Helmo condericto pro sex solid.
tribuat. scuto cum lancia pro duos solid. tribuat." It is doubtful that Brunner
is correct in assuming that this list of values for the above can be viewed
as a list of the national arms of the Ripuarian Franks.

115

an early seventh-century compilation of this law code providing the same list upon which the revolutionary thesis rests.[10] Brunner's failure to use all available historical evidence and his misuse of the Ripuarian code undermine the validity of his argument.

The weaknesses of Brunner's theory, at least in part, were grasped by some of the scholars who have contended that there was a gradual development of mounted warfare under the Merovingian kings. Perhaps the most articulate spokesman for this position is Charles Oman whose *History of the Art of War in the Middle Ages* appeared in 1898.[11] Although Oman accepts the concept, formulated by Brunner and based upon Byzantine sources, of the Merovingian army as a levy of half-naked Franks, he holds this view to be valid only through the sixth and part of the seventh century at which time he sees the gradual development of a cavalry force. In defending Brunner's account of the Merovingian military for the era of Clovis and his sons, Oman argues that the Franks had changed little from the days of Tacitus and "bore a great resemblance to their Sigambrian or Chamavian ancestors. . . ."[12] Apparently Oman believed the Sicambrians had changed their customs radically during the period between Caesar's description of them as a mounted people and the early second century A.D., when Tacitus was silent about their tactics.[13]

Though Oman admits the Romans or Gallo-Romans served in the armies of the Merovingian kings, he maintains "it is quite clear that the conquerors did not adopt the arms of the conquered, and that the survival of Roman garb and weapons among the Gauls disappeared in the sixth century." He remarks further that "they [the Franks] seemed to have borrowed nothing from their Roman predecessors."[14] Oman does not indicate the nature

[10] R. Buchner, "Die Rechtsquellen," *Wattenbach-Levison Deutschlands Geschichtsquellen im Mittelalter* (Weimar, 1953), pp. 23ff.
[11] London, 1898. A second and expanded edition in two volumes appeared in 1923. All citations here are to the 1923 edition. Oman published an earlier essay entitled *The Art of War in the Middle Ages* (Oxford, 1885).
[12] *Art of War*, I, 51–52.
[13] Caesar, *B.G.*, VI, 35, quoted in ch. I, n. 36.
[14] *Art of War*, I, 53; cf. 54.

CONCLUSION

of the evidence which would clarify this conclusion and ignores the evidence to the contrary.

Oman's primary purpose is not to demonstrate the Frankish nature of the Merovingian armies or the lack of imperial influence, but rather to show how a group of primitive Franks became the heavily armed knights of European chivalry. To demonstrate the gradual nature of this change, Oman begins by citing an instance of Franks fighting on horseback in 539 and provides a host of such examples up through the first third of the seventh century.[15] For some unknown reason he neglects Gregory's reference to a Frankish cavalry charge in 531, as well as accounts from the last century of Merovingian history, except for the battle of Poitiers, at which, he grudgingly admits, Charles Martel's troops fought on foot. He does contend that such a tactic was very unusual by then.[16]

The most comprehensive effort to illustrate the gradual development and expansion of the use of heavily armed horsemen in Gaul from approximately 500 to 900 is Hans von Mangoldt-Gaudlitz's *Die Reiterei in den germanischen und fränkischen Heeren bis zum Ausgang der deutschen Karolinger* which appeared in 1922. According to von Mangoldt-Gaudlitz, the fighting forces of early medieval Europe were Germanic and they evolved from the various tribes which conquered the Roman empire. He devotes his first chapter to the German military from its initial appearance in history to the end of Roman rule in Gaul, arguing that some groups customarily fought on horseback whereas others were generally infantry-oriented.[17] In order for the Franks, or presumably for any group of infantry people, to develop an out-

[15] *Ibid.*, I, 54ff.
[16] *Ibid.*, I, 58. Gustav Roloff, "Die Umwandlung des fränkischen Heers von Chlodoweg bis Karl den Grossen," *Neue Jahrbücher für das klassische Altertum*, IX (1902), 389–399, is also of gradualist persuasion. On pp. 390–391, n. 1, Roloff contends that Brunner's interpretation of the evidence for the battle of Poitiers is wrong. He also argues against Brunner's interpretation of the accounts given by Procopius and Agathias. In doing so, Roloff attacks by implication Oman's acceptance of the Byzantine authors, as well as his treatment of Isidore's continuator on Poitiers.
[17] Berlin, 1922, pp. 3–12. "Die zeit von dem ersten Auftreten der Germanen in der Geschichte bis zu dem Untergang der Römerherrschaft in Gallien."

117

standing cavalry two conditions, asserts von Mangoldt-Gaudlitz, were necessary: the economic means to support large numbers of horsemen, and an enemy which could be combated effectively only on horseback. Basing his interpretation on these two pre-requisites, he concludes that as the Franks came to dominate more territory they obtained the means to support a greater num-ber of horsemen; at the same time the Franks found it ncessary to fight against the Visigoths, Avars, Lombards, and Muslims, all of whom, he maintains, fought on horseback and against whom the Franks could be decisive only as cavalrymen. Having thus defined the problem and the framework for its solution, von Mangoldt-Gaudlitz tries to demonstrate the gradual development of horsemen among the Franks by listing instances in which fighting forces of the Merovingian kings and magnates are noted as appearing in battle or some paramilitary operation on horse-back.[18] He then makes a similar catalog for the Carolingian period. This statistical exercise is completed by counting the instances of mounted Merovingian and Carolingian units men-tioned in the sources selected. He concludes that since the refer-ence to horsemen gradually increased throughout the period (500–900) in rough proportion to both Frankish expansion and Frankish wars against mounted enemies, then the number of horsemen increased also.[19]

The diverse nature and varying quantity and quality of the source materials of the early Middle Ages invalidate von Man-goldt-Gaudlitz's statistical method which is based upon the as-sumption that the surviving notices of equestrian activity in the limited number of selected sources are a representatively bal-anced sample of the whole. These criticisms of von Mangoldt-Gaudlitz's statistical method may not, however, convince the less mathematically oriented reader of the work's weaknesses. For those who would defend von Mangoldt-Gaudlitz's work it should be noted that he devotes only thirteen pages to the written sources of the Merovingian period, disregards much of the evi-

[18] Von Mangoldt-Gaudlitz, *Reiterei*, pp. 13–20, and 49.
[19] *Ibid.*, pp. 21–25, and 25–49. The archaeological evidence is used in a similar manner, pp. 65, 67–73.

CONCLUSION

Alfons Dopsch, whose work is an unremitting effort to show continuity between the late empire and the Middle Ages, recognized in Brunner's arguments a dangerous threat to his own historical position. As Brunner's most tenacious critic, Dopsch devoted about six pages of his two-volume *Wirtschaftliche und Soziale Grundlagen der Europäischen Kulturentwicklung aus der Zeit von Caesar bis auf Karl den Grossen* to the Merovingian military, arguing that the Germanic tribes, and especially the Franks, had mounted troops in substantial numbers and of fine quality. To prove this, Dopsch cites a number of texts ignored by Brunner, and even some ignored by the gradualists, which indicate the existence of forces of the Merovingian kings serving on horseback.[26] Dopsch also uses the researches of Erban, Fehr, and Rubel to contend that levies of freemen fighting on foot continued to be of importance in the Carolingian era. Thus, in his opinion, the military in the Merovingian era was predominantly infantry, though horsemen were of considerable significance, and he sees the situation largely unchanged during the Carolingian period.[27]

In response to more than a half-century of criticism directed against Brunner, C. von Schwerin and H. Voltini came to his support, but in doing so fundamentally altered his original

---

lemagne's reign a substantial part of the army was composed of horsemen. In describing this process he writes: ". . . dass er ins achten Jahrhundert hinaufreiche, weil bereits die Heere Karls des Grossen zum guten Theile aus Reiterei bestanden hätten" (p. 7).

The Erban-Fehr interpretation is criticized in an important article by Heinrich Dannenbauer, "Die Freien im karolingische Heer," *Aus Verfassungs- und Landesgeschichte: Festschrift für T. Mayer* (Lindau, 1954), I, 49–64.

[26] Vienna, 1920, II, 292–297.

[27] Dopsch, *Grundlagen der europäischen Kulturentwicklung*, pp. 297–299. H. A. Cronne, "The Origins of Feudalism," *History*, XXIV (1939), 257, finds Dopsch's arguments "not a little bewildering, and to some extent mutually destructive." It seems rather that Cronne misunderstands Dopsch. White, *Med. Tech.*, p. 5, is also bewildered, and believes that when Cronne made the remark above, he was referring to "military historians who deny that the second quarter of the eighth century witnessed any decisive change in methods of fighting." Dopsch, on the contrary, seems to be arguing that these positions are not mutually destructive and can be brought into harmony.

thesis.[28] Brunner's most recent defender, Lynn White, Jr., suc-
cinctly summarizes the new version of the Brunner thesis on the
Merovingian military. White and Brunner's other adherents ad-
mit that in regard to numbers, levies of free Frankish footmen
were preponderant in both the Merovingian and Carolingian
period. Here the arguments of Erban, Fehr, and Rubel seem to
prevail and Brunner's defenders discard any notion of a revolu-
tion in the conversion of the numerically superior infantry force
in the Merovingian era into a numerically superior cavalry force
by Charles Martel or his successors. Because those who have tried
to justify Brunner's interpretation accept as true the idea that the
"Merovingians fought to some extent on horseback, . . ." they
seem to have succumbed to Dopsch's position — the infantry
remained predominant throughout both the Merovingian and
Carolingian eras, yet both periods witnessed the use of calvary
forces as well. Brunner's defenders would not accept such a
conclusion, however, for they contend that although infantry
levies of ill-armed and ill-disciplined Franks were the "tactically
decisive" arm in the Merovingian military, Charles Martel revolu-
tionized warfare by making the cavalry the decisive military
arm.[29] This picture continues to prevail in the historiography at
present, but neither Brunner nor his adherents ever examined the
military campaigns of Charles Martel and Peppin III in detail.
Such an investigation demonstrates conclusively that cavalry was
not the tactically decisive element of the Merovingian military
under the last two mayors of the palace.[30]

A modern study deserving special notice is Jean-Pierre Bodmer's *Der Krieger der Merowingerzeit*, which may be characterized in German as a work of "historische Anthropologie," and
may be translated into American jargon as "historical sociology."
Bodmer's aim is to describe the world of the Merovingian warrior

[28] Von Schwerin in his edition of Brunner's *Deutsche Rechtsgeschichte*
(Munich, 1928), II, 277, n. 30, and 279, n. 33, and Voltini, "Prekarie und
Beneficium," *Vierteljahrschrift für Sozial und Wirtschaftsgeschichte*, XVI
(1923), 293–305.
[29] White, *Med. Tech.*, pp. 3, 5, 6, 11, 13, 137, 138.
[30] Bullough, "*Europae Pater*," pp. 84–90, and Bachrach, "Charles Martel,"
pp. 49–75, for a critique of the Brunner thesis and its modern defenders.

in his role as a fighting man within the framework of social institutions. Though this effort is noteworthy for its attempt to relate modern sociological techniques to early medieval life, Bodmer bases his work on the assumptions set forth in the historical studies discussed above. This may help to explain why Bodmer limits his study to the period from 481 to 639 and omits more than a century of the Merovingian era. Bodmer is in the unenviable position of writing a work of historical sociology in which his sociological investigations and insights, no matter how fruitful, are severely handicapped by the inadequate historical studies upon which he has been forced to rely.[31]

As has been seen, the most influential works on the Merovingian military have been distortingly selective in their use of evidence and chronologically limited in their choice of subject matter. These previous historical interpretations have been determined by two significant trends. The first concentrates upon the Franks as an ethnic group and equates their military institutions with those of the entire Merovingian military establishment. For the most part scholars have been satisfied with this oversimplification of the Merovingian military organization in which half-naked levies of poorly armed and ill-disciplined Frankish infantrymen, depicted as the numerically preponderant and tactically decisive military element, performed military service because of some putative Teutonic duty.[32] The second trend

[31] Zurich, 1957, pp. 9–14. Bodmer discusses the value of previous works and admits that the Merovingian period has been badly treated: "In den meisten dieser Werker spielt die Merowingerzeit die Rolle einen Stiefkindes." Nevertheless, Bodmer relies heavily on at least three of these works, and says of Delbrück's study: "Delbrücks Geschichte der Kriegskunst enthält neben der leidigen Polemik doch so viel Gutes, dass sich di Benützung dieses Werkes stets empfiehlt."

[32] A recent historical conference produced two massive volumes on military matters in the early Middle Ages; *Ordinamenti Militari in Occidente nell 'Alto Medioevo* (*Settimane di Studio del Centro Italiano di Studi sull 'Alto Medioevo*, XV [Spoleto, 1968]). Of the many studies which appear in these volumes only one, Joachim Werner, "Bewaffnung und Waffenbeigabe in der Merowingerzeit," I, 95–108, deals with military organization in Merovingian Gaul in even a limited manner. This essay is devoted essentially to Frankish weapons. In their expansion on Schmidt's work, Zölner (with J. Werner), *Geschichte der Franken*, pp. 150–167, provide no conceptual innovation.

123

focuses upon the means and circumstances by which these primitive warriors were developed into a heavily armed feudal cavalry that is alleged to have dominated the battlefields of medieval Europe and to have formed the basis of the nobility.[33]

A study of all the significant texts relating to Merovingian military organization refutes these widely accepted interpretations, and from such an examination a far different picture emerges. When Clovis died in 511, he left his sons a military establishment which owed much to the empire. Fortified cities and *castra* were garrisoned by erstwhile imperial military personnel (*milites* and *laeti*) and their descendants. Gallo-Roman magnates, both lay and ecclesiastical, were the sworn followers (*leudes*) of the Merovingian monarchs; they were a formidable force in local affairs and their loyalty was essential to a successful reign. Throughout the lands of the royal fisc — much of which had been the imperial fisc and upon which Roman military colonists had been settled — Clovis organized *centenae* or garrison settlements of Franks and others who, as sworn members of the king's *trustis*, served in military and paramilitary actions. The king also kept a large group of armed men at his side, usually called *pueri* in the sources, who were also probably members of his *trustis*.

Clovis's sons changed little of what they inherited. The magnates, both Gallo-Romans and Franks and their supporters, played a large role in military operations during their reigns, as did garrisons in fortified positions. The heterogeneous ethnic composition of the Merovingian military, including Alamans, Alans, Taifals, and Saxons, as well as Gallo-Romans and Franks, was expanded by Clovis's sons with the inclusion of the Burgundians and their military establishment. This acquisition brought the Merovingian kings not only fortresses, fortified cities, garrisons, magnates and their followers, but a standing army, probably of imperial origin, which served under the patrician of Burgundy who was usually of Gallo-Roman origin.

Under Clovis's grandsons a great innovation was introduced into Merovingian military organization — the local levy. Through

[33] White, *Med. Tech.*, pp. 1–38.

these local levies, which were established only in the cities of Neustria and Aquitaine during this period, Clovis's grandsons were able to mobilize much larger numbers of fighting men on a regular basis than had been previously possible. The wars of the latter part of the sixth century also saw the occasional use of general levies which included *pauperes* and *inferiores*.

The last of the ruling Merovingians built upon the work of their predecessors. Local levies were developed in less Romanized parts of Gaul like Mainz and the Saintois. A territorial levy, similar to the territorial levy of Champagne which had been developed during the era of Clovis's grandsons, was organized in Austrasia during this period. Gregory of Tours, whose historical account provides the bulk of the evidence for the reigns of Clovis, his sons, and his grandsons, ceased writing in the last decade of the sixth century at which time the writings of Fredegar and his continuator become the basic source for the Merovingian military. Despite some differences in terminology brought about by the change in authors, the continuity in the Merovingian military through the reign of Dagobert I remains clear.

The era of the *rois fainéants* and the mayors of the palace marks some noteworthy changes in Merovingian military organization. In Austrasia especially, the various types of levies fade out of existence before the middle of the seventh century and military force is left in the hands of the magnates and their armed followers. The military in Neustria and Burgundy experienced the same kind of change, but in Aquitaine, the most Romanized part of Gaul, more complex forms of military organization including garrisons, levies, and the magnates with their followings survive.

Throughout the last century of Merovingian history, the magnates and their armed supporters became the primary military forces in most of Gaul. This is not to say that the number of magnates or even the number of their armed followers increased for no evidence concerning numbers is to be found. The magnates and their retainers grew more important militarily during this period because other segments of the military in Merovingian Gaul ceased to exist.

Despite the increasing significance of the magnates' followings, the mayors of the palace continued the same techniques used by the Merovingian kings in acquiring the support of these groups. Gifts in movable wealth and estates were provided by mayors like Aega and Peppin III as they had been by kings like Clovis, Theuderic I, or Dagobert I. Charles Martel, who is alleged to have introduced revolutionary changes, did no more and no less in his efforts to acquire and maintain the support of the magnates and their followers than had his predecessors.[34]

Although previous historical interpretations maintain that the Merovingian forces were poorly armed with only axes and barbed spears, it can be justly concluded that the heterogeneous elements of the Merovingian military used various kinds of weapons. For example, the magnates in Merovingian Gaul provided their followers with mail coats, helmets, shields, lances, swords, bows and arrows, and horses. These retainers resembled in armament the followers of the Gallo-Roman *potentiores* who had flourished under the empire. The remnants of the imperial military who were absorbed into the Merovingian military continued to use their old armor and weapons, and among Rome's erstwhile allies integrated into the Merovingian military, the Alan cavalry so dominated the military of Armorica that their influence was recognizable there at least into the tenth century and probably into the twelfth century.

The local levies of the Neustrian and Aquitanian cities seem to have been well armed with, among other things, defensive armor and mounts. Because the elements of lesser social and economic status (*pauperes* and *inferiores*) which were included in the general levies seem to have been poorly equipped and fought with anything which might come to hand, the general levies were infrequently used and of little military value. The armament of the trans-Rhenish peoples, who were at times called upon for military aid, was little affected by conditions in the West, and they were generally less well armed than members of the same ethnic groups who had fallen under more direct imperial

[34] Bachrach, "Charles Martel," pp. 66–72.

influence. Among the rank and file of the Saxon, Frankish, or Wendish hordes raised beyond the Rhine, body armor was generally lacking; the sword, spear, and ax served as offensive weapons, and horsemen were generally few in number.

The tactics of the Merovingian armies varied from situation to situation and were dictated, in part, by what may perhaps be characterized as Merovingian strategy. The fundamental principle of Merovingian strategy within Gaul was the acquisition and defense of as many fortified cities and *castra* as possible. Outside of Gaul — south of the Alps and Pyrenees — Merovingian strategy generally seems to have been limited to raiding for booty and acquiring tribute. These were also the military goals, at least in part, of Merovingian operations east of the Rhine, although the main intention here was to extend actual political power beyond the Rhine through military activity.

A primary aim of the Merovingian kings and later of the mayors was the control of wealth, which explains in part their interest in maintaining possession of the cities throughout Gaul. For they were the organizational centers of much wealth: lay and ecclesiastical administrations were based in the cities; taxes and tolls were collected there; and markets and merchants flourished. The cities were walled and defensible and with their surrounding area they formed a miniature state to which the local inhabitants even had a particularistic loyalty. The Merovingian kings placed garrisons in these cities; these forces differed organizationally from the local levies and from the general populace and served under commanders different from those who led the local levies.

Warfare throughout the Merovingian era, especially in the more Romanized parts of Gaul — Aquitaine, Neustria, and Burgundy — focused on these walled cities. From Clovis's siege of Paris in the 480s to Charles Martel's siege of Avignon in 737, the investment of fortified positions, whether walled cities or garrisoned *castra*, dominated Merovingian warfare. The Roman origin of this city-oriented aspect of Merovingian strategy and the tactics of siege warfare which necessarily evolved from it cannot be too strongly emphasized. The use of siege engines of various types and the techniques for cutting off provisions and communications, as well as the means of controlling the population in areas surrounding besieged positions and of supplying the besieging forces, though organized to varying degrees and applied with widely differing results, mark the Roman nature of Merovingian warfare both tactically and strategically.

Siege warfare was not the only tactic of the Merovingian military which owed a debt to the empire. The organization of naval forces, such as that which defeated the Danes in 515, and the utilization of river craft for military and paramilitary maneuvers of the Loire, Rhine, and Rhone suggest imperial rather than Frankish influence. In many battles of the Merovingian era which did not involve siege or water operations, tactics seem to have been flexible and dictated more by the demands of a particular situation than by tribal custom. If the tactics of the Merovingian military may be characterized, perhaps the only suitable term would be *flexible*. Siege warfare, mounted attacks, naval operations, and infantry movements were all employed by Merovingian armed forces. Mounted troops, which seem to have been comparatively numerous (even important elements of the local levies were probably mounted), were not committed to fighting on horseback and if the situation were appropriate they dismounted and fought on foot.

The Merovingian military was formed from many peoples and groups, its tactics were flexible, and its strategy was variable. Perhaps the most important conclusion that can be drawn from the present study, especially in light of previous scholarship, is that the Merovingian military was greatly influenced by the Roman empire and its institutions, and it owed comparatively little to the Franks, who were only a minority of the population and a small part of the fighting forces. As with many aspects of Merovingian life, the military organization recalls *Romania* and not *Germania*.

Appendix

The Byzantines' View
of the Franks

THE FRANKS, though a minority of the population in Gaul, did play a part in the Merovingian armies. For generations, however, historians have accepted the descriptions of Frankish tactics and armament given by the Byzantine writers Procopius and Agathias as the basis for understanding the entire Merovingian military establishment.[1] A careful study of these texts suggests they should be reevaluated.[2] Toward the middle of the sixth century Procopius wrote concerning the Franks:

> At this time [539] the Franks, hearing that both the Goths and Romans had suffered severely by the war . . . forgetting for the moment their oaths and treaties . . . (for this nation [ἔθνος] in matters of trust is the most treacherous in the world), they straightway gathered to the number of one hundred thousand under the leadership of Theudebert, and marched into Italy: they had a small body of cavalry about their leader, and these were the only ones armed with spears [δόρατα], while all the rest were foot

---

[1] Bachrach, "Procopius, Agathias, and the Frankish Military," pp. 435–436.

[2] The only specific criticism of these texts and their defenders appears in a footnote by Gustav Roloff, "Die Umwandlung des fränkischen Heers," p. 392, n. 1. Walter Goffart, "Byzantine Policy," p. 77, n. 12, maintains that Agathias's descriptive chapters on the Franks contain outrageous errors. In this he follows E. Cougny, *Extraits des auteurs grecs concernant la géographie et l'histoire des Gaules*, V (Société de l'histoire de France [Paris, 1866], 415, n. 1). Unfortunately, neither author comments on Agathias's description of the Franks' military tactics and armament. Cf. A. Cameron, "How Did the Merovingian Kings Wear Their Hair?" *RBPH*, XLIII (1965), 1208, and "Agathias on the Early Merovingians," pp. 130–132, 139–140.

soldiers having neither bows nor spears [δόρατα], but each man carried a sword and shield and one axe. Now the iron head of this weapon was thick and exceedingly sharp on both sides, while the wooden handle was very short. And they are accustomed always to throw these axes at one signal in the first charge and thus to shatter the shields of the enemy and kill the men.[3]

Some two decades after Procopius gave this account, Agathias wrote:

The military equipment of this people [ἔθνος] is very simple. . . . They do not know the use of the coat of mail or greaves and the majority leave the head uncovered, only a few wear the helmet. They have their chests bare and backs naked to the loins, they cover their thighs with either leather or linen. They do not serve on horseback except in very rare cases. Fighting on foot is both habitual and a national [πάτριον] custom and they are proficient in this. At the hip they wear a sword and on the left side their shield is attached. They have neither bows nor slings, no missile weapons except the double edged axe and the angon [ἄγγωνας] which they use most often. The angons are spears [δόρατα] which are neither very short nor very long; they can be used, if necessary, for throwing like a javelin, and also, in hand to hand combat. The greater part of the angon is covered with iron and very little wood is exposed. Above, at the top of the spear, on each side from the socket itself where the staff is fixed, some points are turned back, bent like hooks and turned toward the handle. In battle, the Frank throws the angon, and if it hits an enemy the spear is caught in the man and neither the wounded man nor anyone else can draw it out. The barbs hold inside the flesh causing great pain and in this way a man whose wound may not be in a vital spot still dies. If the angon strikes a shield, it is fixed there, hanging down with the butt on the ground. The angon cannot be pulled out because the barbs have penetrated the shield, nor can it be cut off with a sword because the wood of the shaft is covered with iron. When the Frank sees the situation, he quickly puts his foot on the butt of the spear, pulling down and the man holding it falls, the head and chest are left unprotected. The unprotected warrior is then killed either by a stroke of the axe or a thrust with another spear [δόρατι]. Such is the equipment of the Frankish warriors. . . .[4]

[3] Procopius, *H.W.*, VI, xxv, 3ff.
[4] Agathias, *Hist.*, II, 5.

APPENDIX

Although it is clear that Agathias is giving a general description of Frankish armament and tactics, it is less obvious in Procopius's case. Procopius begins by characterizing the army that Theudebert led into Italy in 539, but he soon makes his account a general one with a portrayal of the Frankish ax and tactics "always" (ἀεί) used by the Franks. It is not unfair to argue that Procopius, as well as Agathias, intended to describe Frankish military customs in general rather than the armament and tactics of a particular army in a particular campaign. Though Procopius, as a member of Belisarius's staff in Italy, may have had the opportunity to obtain information from men who had faced the Franks in battle in 539, there is no evidence to support this. By providing his readers with a grossly exaggerated figure for the size of Theudebert's army, Procopius casts doubt upon the accuracy of his remarks in this passage.

Procopius asserts that the Frankish infantry, which he contends made up the vast majority of Theudebert's army, do not carry a spear (δόρυ), while Agathias argues that the *ango,* which he classes as a spear (δόρυ), is the Frankish foot soldier's primary weapon and spends almost two-thirds of his description demonstrating how the weapon is used and why it is so effective. Agathias's account may even indicate that at least some Frankish footmen carried more than one spear: the *ango* mentioned above and a spear (δόρυ) used for thrusting. In yet another context Aagthias portrays Frankish infantry using a javelin (ἀκόντιον).[5] Although Procopius does not mention the *ango,* he maintains that the throwing ax is the Frankish infantryman's key weapon, and his description of its construction and use dominates his account of Frankish tactics and armaments. Agathias also classifies the Franks' ax as a missile weapon, but he pictures it as a hand weapon as well.

A study of the archaeological evidence is of little help in clarifying the use of weapons since Frankish graves yield not only *angos* and axes, but a variety of spearheads.[6] Sidonius Apollinaris, writing during the second half of the fifth century, states that the Franks used the ax and also the *ango* (*lancea uncata*). Is it possible that Sidonius's pedantic letter to his friend Domnicius, a military buff who was "fond of looking at arms and armed

---

[5] *Ibid.,* I, 15.
[6] Salin, *Civ. mérov.,* I, 356, 377, 385, 389, for *angos;* III, 23ff, for axes; and 13ff, for a variety of spears. Werner, "Bewaffnung und Waffenbeigabe," pl. V, shows that the distribution of *ango*-finds are east of the Rhine which strongly suggests that the Franks whom Agathias describes were not recruited from Merovingian lands but from trans-Rhenish areas.

men," served as a basis for Procopius's and Agathias's narratives written about a century later? Although Sidonius offers an account of Frankish warriors in battle, he does not confirm the tactical formations described by Procopius and Agathias. Sidonius demonstrates that the Frankish footmen used not only the barbed spear, but a spear (*hasta*) which does not seem to have been barbed.[7] The importance of the spear to the Frankish footman, as indicated by Libanius during the previous century, is of course denied by Procopius.[8]

Gregory of Tours, who was much closer in proximity to the Franks and much closer in time to Procopius and Agathias than was Sidonius, describes many battles in which Franks took part, but he does not confirm the tactics described by either Procopius or Agathias. Gregory pictures the Franks using their axes on five separate occasions. In only one case, however, is the ax characterized as being thrown; in the other instances it is used as a hand weapon. Gregory does not deal with the strong points of the *ango* as Agathias does — in fact he does not even mention it, although he often writes about spears being used. The written sources and the archaeological evidence indicate that the short sword (*scramasax*) was a significant Frankish weapon, yet neither Procopius nor Agathias seems to know of its existence.[9]

Procopius and Agathias do concur on several points. They both maintain that the Franks did not use the bow. Gregory of Tours, however, who probably knew more about the Franks than did his Byzantine contemporaries, disagrees with them on this point, quoting Sulpicius Alexander to the effect that the Franks had used the bow since at least the fourth century. The archaeological evidence confirms Gregory's view, for numerous arrowheads have been found in Frankish graves.[10] Procopius and Agathias also agree that horesmen were unimportant among the Franks. According to Procopius, the Franks had a very few horsemen gathered about their leader, and Agathias claims that the Franks served on horseback only on rare occasions. Both these descrip-

[7] Sidonius Apollinaris, *Ep.*, 4, 20, and *Pan.*, 5, 247ff.

[8] Libanius, *oratio*, lix, 275.

[9] Gregory, *Hist.*, IX, 35, for the ax being thrown; two instances in II, 27; VII, 14, VIII, 19, for the ax being used as a hand weapon. For spears of all kinds, IV, 30, V, 32, IX, 10, III, 14, V, 25, VII, 29; and for the scramasax, IV, 51. For the importance of the scramasax see H. Althoff, *Waltharii Poesis* (Leipzig, 1905), pp. 376–377, and Salin, *Civ. mérov.*, III, 45ff.

[10] Gregory, *Hist.*, V, 20; V, 48; X, 16; and for the quotation from Sulpicius, II, 9. For arrowheads in Frankish graves, Salin, *Civ. mérov.*, I, 356, and II, 87, 239, 241.

tions, however, are relative judgments; what may be a small number to one observer may well be considered a large number by another, whereas what might be a rare occasion to one might seem reasonably frequent to another. The observer's norm or basis for calculation determines such judgments and the norm of the classical world was one horseman to every ten footmen.[11] For the Byzantine army of the mid-sixth century, field forces seem to have been about fifty percent infantry and fifty percent cavalry. It should also be noted that for contemporaries, the Byzantine cavalry was the core of the army, and the infantry played an insignificant role.[12] Seen in light of their norm, Procopius and Agathias may well have thought that horsemen were few among the Franks or rarely used by them. In lieu of any more definite data (if Procopius and Agathias are to be trusted on this point at all) the sole conclusion that can be drawn is that horsemen were of less importance to the Franks as an ethnic group than they were to the Byzantines. There is, however, substantial information about Frankish military customs from which a much different interpretation emerges. Agathias himself writes of a small battle near Rimini in 554, in which the Byzantines fought against a force of some 2000 Franks, about half of whom were horsemen.[13] Perhaps this was one of those rare occasions when, according to Agathias, the Franks fought on horseback.

In 531 Theuderic I and Chlotar I led an expedition of what seems to have been purely Frankish warriors into Thuringia and sought out the main force of the enemy. Shortly before the two armies were to engage, the Thuringians managed to maneuver the Franks into what they hoped would be a disadvantageous position. They dug pits in a field and covered them with sod so that the approaching Frankish horsemen would be unaware of the trap. When the Franks charged across the field to meet the Thuringians, their horses were tripped up by the ditches so that they were slowed down and almost had to turn back.[14]

The elaborate preparations made by the Thuringians suggest that they had had some previous experience with Frankish cavalry; because they expected the Franks to be on horseback, they had to devise plans to combat their mounted tactics. The Thuringians may well have learned the capabilities of the Frankish

[11] J. K. Anderson, *Ancient Greek Horsemanship* (Berkeley, 1961), p. 141.
[12] Bury, *Later Roman Empire*, II, 77–78, 85, 132, 136ff. Robert Grosse, *Römische Militärgeschichte vom Gallienus bis zum Beginn der byzantinischen Themenverfassung* (Berlin, 1928), pp. 283ff, and 313ff.
[13] Agathias, *Hist.*, I, 21.
[14] Gregory, *Hist.*, III, 7.

horsemen some fifteen years earlier when Theuderic intervened quite successfully in one of their civil wars.[15] Gregory of Tours relates the story of the charge of Frankish horsemen in detail without a word of surprise concerning their equestrian tactics. Gregory, of course, lived in Gaul and was probably accustomed to seeing Frankish horsemen. The Thuringians certainly were not surprised by the Franks' use of horsemen in 531; indeed they had prepared for it. It is difficult to say how Procopius and Agathias would have reacted had they witnessed this battle.

Horsemen also seem to have been an important element of Clovis's army. Before his campaign against the Visigoths in 507, Clovis issued specific orders to his troops concerning the taking of fodder and water for their mounts. Although these commands may well have been meant primarily for his Armorican allies (among whom were a significant number of Alan horsemen), it was apparently an unimportant Frank — not a noble or royal bodyguard — who was executed for violating the orders.[16] To support further the conclusion that cavalrymen played a significant role in Clovis's forces, it should be recalled that Clovis and his followers were identified by at least one comparatively well-informed contemporary as descendants of the Sicambri who were well known for their equestrian prowess.[17] Clovis's father, Childeric, was so equestrian-oriented that he had the head of his warhorse entombed with him at Tournai.[18] The Franks of the fifth and even the fourth centuries had gained such a reputation for their horsemanship that they were recruited by the empire for cavalry regiments. Of the four primarily Frankish units listed in the *Notitia Dignitatum* in approximately 425, all were cavalry regiments.[19]

Although Frankish equestrian prowess seems to have been ignored in the East, it was widely recognized in the West. Rabanus Maurus quotes a common Frankish proverb to the effect that one must begin at puberty if one is to become an effective horseman.[20] Einhard asserts that the chase and equestrian exercises were Frankish national customs.[21] What some scholars con-

[15] *Ibid.*, III, 4.
[16] *Ibid.*, II, 37.
[17] Caesar, *B.G.*, VI, 35.
[18] Cf. Wallace-Hadrill, *Long-Haired Kings*, p. 162.
[19] See ch. I, n. 33.
[20] Rabanus Maurus, *De procinctu Romanae miliciae*, p. 3: "Unde et vulgaricum proverbium ac nostris familiare est quod dicitur: in pube posse fieri equitem, majoris vero aetatis aut vix aut numquam."
[21] Einhard, *V. Karoli*, ch. 22: "Exercebatur adsidue equitando ac venando:

sider the national arms of the Ripuarian Franks are listed in the first extant copy of their law code (about 630), which suggests that the Ripuarians were also horsemen.[22] Equestrian activity among the Salians seems to have equaled that of the Ripuarians. Chlotar II, for example, was as devoted to the chase as Charlemagne.[23] This was also true of Chilperic I, who was killed while dismounting from his horse after returning from the hunt, and of his son Merovech who rode out to the chase despite great dangers.[24]

An abundance of horses, which is a prerequisite for effective cavalry organization, is indicated clearly by the frequent legislation regarding them even in the earliest compilation of the *Lex Salica* (about 510).[25] Horses appear so frequently in the Salian Frankish laws that at least one noted medieval economic historian has been led to contend that the Franks had a great many horses and thus could use them for plowing when everyone else used oxen.[26]

The significance of horses is further illustrated by the elaborate organization of horse-breeding estates under the Merovingian kings. These estates were under the central control of the constable (*comes stabuli*) who was an important member of the royal household. Each estate was administered by a bailiff who in turn supervised numerous wranglers and grooms. Because of their jobs these men seem to have enjoyed a preferred position in society which others of comparable legal or social status, but of different occupational status, did not have.[27]

---

quod illi gentilicium erat, quia vix ulla in terris natio invenitur quae in hac arte Francis possit aequari."

[22] *Lex Rib.*, 40 (36), 11.

[23] Fred., IV, 42: ". . . Chlotharius . . . venacionem ferarum nimium assiduae utens. . . ."

[24] Gregory, *Hist.*, V, 14: "Ait ille praesto putans esse interfectores, ait ad Merovechum: "Ut quid hic quasi signes et timidi resedemus et ut hebetis circa basilicam occulimur? Veniant enim equi nostri, et acceptis accipitribus, cum canibus exerceamur venatione spectaculisque patulis iocundemur.'" VI, 46: "Quadam vero die regressus de venatione iam sub obscura nocte, dum de equo susceperitur et unam manu super scapulam pueri reteniret, adveniens quidam eum cultro percutit sub ascellam iteratoque ictu ventrem eius perforat; statimque profluente cupia sanguinis tam per os quam per aditum vulneris, iniquum fudit spiritum."

[25] *Lex Sal.*, 9, 1; 10, 1; 23; 27, 3–5; 37, 15; 38, 1 and 3, 6 [7, 8]; 47, 1; 65, 1.

[26] Charles Edmond Perain, "The Evolution of Agricultural Technique," *The Cambridge Economic History*, ed. M. Postan et al., 2nd ed. (Cambridge, 1966), I, 142.

[27] Fustel de Coulanges, *Hist. des inst.*, IV, 148–149. Gregory, *Hist.*, III, 15; V, 39; VIII, 40; IX, 38; and Gregory, *G.M.*, I, 29.

If Procopius's and Agathias's remarks concerning the horsemen of the Franks are understood as meaning that they had a number of horsemen so inconsequential as to be hardly worth notice, then the Byzantine writers and their interpreters are surely mistaken. If, on the other hand, their comments are taken to imply that horsemen were of less importance to the Franks than to the Byzantines, then they are probably correct. The thrust of the evidence, however, seems to indicate that the Franks had a relatively significant body of horsemen within the Merovingian military establishment.

The utilization of Procopius's and Agathias's judgments concerning Frankish armament and tactics would seem to require more caution than has been usual heretofore. If one were to insist that Procopius's description was of a specific force in a particular campaign, the danger of generalizing about the Frankish military from it is manifest. If, however, Procopius's account is a general one, as argued here, then its defenders must realize that he and Agathias contradict each other as decisively as both are contradicted by sources closer to events and presumably better informed.

Though both Byzantine authors list weapons that were surely used by the Franks, the tactics they characterize are otherwise unconfirmed. It must be made very clear that Procopius's and Agathias's narratives are only of limited value for the study of the Franks as an ethnic group and of no value if used as a description of the heterogeneous Merovingian military.

Bibliography

Bibliography

Primary Sources

Agathias Myrinaei Historiarum Libri Quinque, ed. R. Keydell. Berlin, 1967.

Beowulf, 3rd ed., ed. F. Klaeber. Boston, 1951.

Bon. *ep.*: S. *Bonifatii et Lulli espistolae*, ed. M. Tangl. *MGH Ep.*, vol. I. Hannover, 1916.

Caesar, B. G.: C. *Iuli Caesaris Commentarii rerum in Gestarum*, ed. T. Holmes. Oxford, 1914.

Cap. lex Sal. add.: *Pactus Legis Salicae*, ed. K. Eckhardt. *MGH LL.*, vol. IV, pt. 1. Hannover, 1962.

Chron. Caesaraug., s.a.: *Chronicorum Caesaraugustanorum reliquiae a. CCCLV–DLXXXI*, ed. T. Mommsen. *MGH AA.*, vol. XI, reprint. Berlin, 1961.

Chron. Moissiac: Chronicon Moissiacensi, ed. G. Pertz. *MGH SS.*, vol. II. Hannover, 1829.

Einhard, V. *Karoli: Éiginhard, Vie de Charlemagne*, ed. and trans. L. Halphen. Paris, 1923.

Form. Andec.: *Formulae Merowingici et Karolini aevi*, ed. K. Zeumer. *MGH LL.*, vol. V. Hannover, 1886.

Fred.: *Chronicarum quae dicuntur Fredegarii scholastici libri IV*, ed. B. Krusch. *MGH SSRM.*, vol. II. Hannover, 1888.

Fred. con't.: *Chronicarum quae dicunter Fredegarii scholastici libri IV cum Continuationibus*, ed. B. Krusch. *MGH SSRM.*, vol. II. Hannover, 1888.

Gesta Dagoberti, ed. B. Krusch. *MGH SSRM.*, vol. II. Hannover, 1888.

Gesta Francorum, Patrologia Latinae, ed. J. P. Migne, vol. CXXXIX. Paris, 1880.

Gregory, G.M.: *Gregorii episcopi Turonensis, Liber in Gloria Martyrum*, ed. B. Krusch. *MGH SSRM.*, vol. I. Hannover, 1885.

_____, *Hist.*: *Gregorii episcopi Turonensis, Libri Historiarum*, ed. B. Krusch and W. Levison. *MGH SSRM.*, vol. I, pt. 1. Hannover, 1951.

_____, *Virt. S. Mart.*: *Gregorii episcopi Turonensis, Liber I–IV de virtutibus sancti Martini episcopi*, ed. B. Krusch. *MGH SSRM.*, vol. I. Hannover, 1885.

_____, *V.P.*: *Liber vitae patrum*, ed. B. Krusch. *MGH SSRM.*, vol. I. Hannover, 1885.

_____, *Liber de passione et virtutibus Santi Juliani Martyris*, ed. B. Krusch. *MGH SSRM.*, vol. I. Hannover, 1885.

Isid., *Hist. Goth.*: *Isidori Iunioris episcopi Hispalensis, historia Gothorum,*

141

Wandalorum, Sueborum, ad. a DCXXIV, ed. T. Mommsen. *MGH AA.,* vol. XI, reprint. Berlin, 1961.

Isidori continuatio Hispana, ed. T. Mommsen. *MGH AA.,* vol. XI, reprint. Berlin, 1961.

John Biclar: *Johannis abbatis Biclarensis chronica a DLXVII–DXC,* ed. T. Mommsen. *MGH AA.,* vol. XI, reprint. Berlin, 1961.

Jordanes, *Getica: Jordanis, De origine actibus Getarum,* ed. T. Mommsen. *MGH AA.,* vol. V, pt. 1, reprint. Berlin, 1961.

L.B.: Leges Burgundionum, ed. L. De Salis. *MGH LL.,* vol. II. Hannover, 1892.

Lex Rib.: Lex Ribuaria, ed. R. Buchner. *MGH LL.,* vol. III. Hannover, 1954.

Lex Rom. Burg.: Lex Romana Burgundionum, ed. L. De Salis. *MGH LL.,* vol. II. Hannover, 1892.

Lex Sal.: Pactus Legis Salicae, ed. K. Eckhardt. *MGH LL.,* vol. IV, pt. 1. Hannover, 1962.

L.H.F.: Liber Historiae Francorum, ed. B. Krusch. *MGH SSRM.,* vol. II. Hannover, 1888.

Libanius, *oratio: Libanii Opera,* ed. R. Foerster, vol. IV. Leipzig, 1908.

Marculf, *form.: Formulae Merowingici et Karolini aevi,* ed. K. Zeumer. *MGH LL.,* vol. V. Hannover, 1886.

MGH Cap.: Capitularia Regnum Francorum, ed. A. Boretius. *MGH LL.,* vol. II. Hannover, 1883.

Mir. Martini Abbatis: Miracula Martini Abbatis Vertavensis, ed. B. Krusch. *MGH SSRM.,* vol. III. Hannover, 1896.

Notitia Dignitatum utriusque imperii, ed. O. Seeck. Berlin, 1876.

N. Val.: Valentinian III, *Novellae, Codex Theodosianus,* ed. T. Mommsen, vol. II. Berlin, 1905.

Pardessus: *Diplomata Chartae, Epistolae, Leges,* 2 vols., ed. J. M. Pardessus. Reprint. Darmstadt, 1969.

Pass. Leod.: Passio Leudegarii I, ed. B. Krusch. *MGH SSRM.,* vol. V. Hannover, 1916.

Paul, *Hist.: Pauli Diaconi Historia Langobardorum,* ed. L. Bethmann and G. Waitz. *MGH SSRL.,* Hannover, 1878.

Procopius, *H.W.: History of the Wars,* 5 vols., ed. and trans. H. Dewing. London, 1914–1928.

————, *H.W.: Procopius Caesaraensis, Opera,* ed. J. Haury and G. Wirth, vol. II. Leipzig, 1963.

Rabanus Maurus, "De procinctu Romanae miliciae," ed. E. Dümmler, *Zeitschrift für deutschen Altertum,* XV (1872), 443–451.

Sid. Apol.: *Sidonii Apollinaris, Epistulae et Carmina,* ed. C. Luetjohann. *MGH AA.,* vol. VIII. Berlin, 1887.

Tacitus, *Germania,* ed. R. Robinson. Middletown, Conn., 1935.

V. Caes.: Vita Caesarii episcopi Arlatensis, ed. B. Krusch. *MGH SSRM.,* Hannover, 1896.

V. Columbani, ed. B. Krusch. *MGH SSRG.,* Hannover, 1905.

V. Dalmat.: Vita Dalmatii episcopi Ruteni, ed. B. Krusch. *MGH SSRM.,* vol. III. Hannover, 1896.

V. Danielis: Vita S. Danielis Stylitae, ed. H. Delehaye, *Analecta Bollandiana,* XXXII (1913), 121–214.

V. Desid.: Vita S. Desiderii episcopi Viennensis, ed. M. Bouquet, vol. III. Paris, 1869.

BIBLIOGRAPHY

V. Epiphanii, ed. F. Vogel. *MGH AA.,* vol. VII. Berlin, 1885.
V. Eptadii, ed. B. Krusch. *MGH SSRM.,* vol. III. Hannover, 1896.
V. Eucherii, episcopi Aurelianensis, ed. W. Levison. *MGH SSRM.,* vol. VII. Hannover, 1919.
V. Galact.: De S. Galactorio Episcopo Lascurrensi, Act. sanct., vol. XXVII. Paris, Rome, July 1868.
V. Genov.: Vita Genovefae virginis Parisiensis, ed. B. Krusch. *MGH SSRM.,* vol. III. Hannover, 1896.
V. Landiberti, ed. B. Krusch. *MGH SSRM.,* vol. IV. Hannover, 1913.
V. Maximini, ed. B. Krusch. *MGH SSRM.,* vol. III. Hannover, 1896.
V. Remigii, ed. B. Krusch. *MGH SSRM.,* vol. III. Hannover, 1896.
V. Valent.: Vita S. Valenti Presbyteri, ed. M. Bouquet, vol. III. Paris, 1869.
V. Wilfrithi: The Life of Bishop Wilfrid by Eddius Stephanus, ed. and trans. B. Colgrave. Cambridge, 1927.
V. Willibrodi, ed. W. Levison. *MGH SSRM.,* vol. VII. Hannover, 1919.

Secondary Works

Althoff, H. *Waltharii Poesis.* Leipzig, 1905.
Anderson, J. K. *Ancient Greek Horsemanship.* Berkeley, 1961.
Bachrach, Bernard S. "The Alans in Gaul," *Traditio,* XXIII (1967), 476–489.
_____. "Was There Feudalism in Byzantine Egypt?" *Journal of the American Research Center in Egypt,* VI (1967), 163–166.
_____. "A Note on Alites," *Byzantinische Zeitschrift,* LXI (1968), 35.
_____. "Another Look at the Barbarian Settlement in Southern Gaul," *Traditio,* XXV (1969), 354–358.
_____. "The Origin of Armorican Chivalry," *Technology and Culture,* X (1969), 166–171.
_____. "Charles Martel, Mounted Shock Combat, the Stirrup, and Feudalism," *Studies in Medieval and Renaissance History,* VII (1970), 49–75.
_____. "Procopius, Agathias, and the Frankish Military," *Speculum,* XLV (1970), 435–441.
_____. "Procopius and the Chronology of Clovis's Reign," *Viator,* I (1970), 21–31.
_____. "The Feigned Retreat at Hastings," *Mediaeval Studies,* XXXIII (1971), 264–267.
Baudot, M. "Localisation et datation de la première victoire remportée par Charles Martel contre les Musulmans," *Mémoires et documents publiés par la Société de l'École des Chartes,* XII (1955), 93–105.
Bloch, Marc. *Feudal Society.* Trans. L. A. Manyon. London, 1961.
Bodmer, Jean Pierre. *Der Krieger der Merowingerzeit und seiner Welt.* Zurich, 1957.
Boutaric, Edgard. *Institutions militaires de la France avant les armées permanentes.* Paris, 1863.
Brunner, Heinrich. "Die Reiterdienst und die Anfänge des Lehnwesens," *ZRG,* VIII (1887), 1–38.
_____. *Forschungen zur Geschichte des deutschen und französischen Rechts.* Stuttgart, 1894.
_____. *Deutsche Rechtsgeschichte.* 2nd ed. Munich, 1928.
Buchner, R. "Die Rechtsquellen." In *Wattenbach-Levison Deutschlands Geschichtsquellen in Mittelalter.* Weimar, 1953.

Bullough, Donald. "*Europae Pater:* Charlemagne and His Achievement in the Light of Recent Scholarship," *EHR*, LXXV (1970), 84–89.

Bury, J. B. "The Notitia Dignitatum," *JRS*, X (1920), 131–154.

————. *History of the Later Roman Empire.* 2 vols. Dover ed. New York, 1958.

Butler, R. M. "Late Roman Town Walls in Gaul," *The Archaeological Journal*, CXVI (1959), 25–50.

Cam, Helen. *Local Government in Francia and England.* London, 1912.

Cameron, Averil. "How Did the Merovingian Kings Wear Their Hair?" *RBPH*, XLIII (1965), 1203–1216.

————. "Agathias on the Early Merovingians," *Annali della Scuola Normale Superiore di Pisa*, XXXVII (1968), 95–140.

Claude, Dietrich. "Untersuchen zum frühfrankischen Comitat," *ZRG*, LXXXI (1964), 1–79.

Codera, F. "Manusa y el duque Eudon," *Estudios críticos de historia árabe-española.* In *Collección de los estudios árabes*, vol. VII, pp. 140–169. Saragossa, 1903.

Collingwood, R. G., and J. N. L. Myres. *Roman Britain.* 2nd ed. Oxford, 1937.

Cougny, E. *Extraits des auteurs grecs concernant la géographie et l'histoire des Gaules*, vol. V. Société de l'histoire de France, Paris, 1866.

Cronne, A. H. "The Origins of Feudalism," *History*, XXIV (1939), 251–259.

Dalton, O. M. *The History of the Franks by Gregory of Tours.* 2 vols. Oxford, 1927.

Dannenbauer, H. "Die Freien im karolingische Heer." In *Aus Verfassungs- und Landesgeschichte: Festschrift für T. Mayer*, vol. I, pp. 49–64. Lindau, 1954.

Dauzat, A., and C. Rostaing. *Dictionnaire étymologique des noms de lieux en France.* Paris, 1963.

Delbrück, Hans. *Numbers in History.* London, 1913.

————. *Geschichte der Kriegskunst in Rahmen der politischen Geschichte.* 6 vols. 2nd ed. Berlin, 1920–1932.

Deloche, Maximin. *La trustis et l'antrustion royal sous les deux premières races.* Paris, 1873.

Dill, Samuel. *Roman Society in Gaul in the Merovingian Age.* London, 1926.

Dippe, Oskar. *Gefolgschaft und Huldigung im Reiche der Merowinger.* Wandsbeck, 1889.

Doehaerd, R. "La richesse des Mérovingiens." In *Studi in onore di Gino Luzzatto*, vol. I, pp. 30–46. Milan, 1949.

Dopsch, Alfons. *Wirtschaftliche und soziale Grundlagen der europäischen Kulturentwicklung*, 2 vols. 2nd ed. Vienna, 1924.

————. "Die Leudes und das Lehnwesen," *MIÖG*, XLI (1926), 35–43.

————. "Beneficialwesen und Feudalität," *MIÖG*, XLVI (1932), 1–36.

Dupraz, Louis. *Contribution a l'histoire du Regnum Francorum.* Fribourg, 1948.

Erban, W. "Zur Geschichte des karolingischen Kriegswesens," *HZ*, CI (1908), 321–336.

Ewig, Eugen. "Die fränkischen Teilungen und Teilreiche (511–613)," *Akademie der Wissenschaften und der Literatur*, IX (1952), 651–715.

————. "Die fränkischen Teilreiche im 7 Jahrhundert (613–714)," *Trierer Zeitschrift*, XXII (1953), 85–144.

Fehr, H. "Das Waffenrecht der Bauern im Mittelalter," *ZRG*, XXXV (1914), 111–211.

BIBLIOGRAPHY

Fischer, K. *The Burgundian Code*. Philadelphia, 1949.
Frauenholz, Eugen von. *Das Heerwesen der germanischen Frühzeit*. Munich, 1935.
Freeman, E. A. *Western Europe in the Eighth Century and Onward*. London, 1904.
Fuller, J. F. C. *The Decisive Battles of the Western World*. 3 vols. London, 1954–1956.
Fustel de Coulanges, N. D. *Histoire des institutions politiques de l'ancienne France*. 6 vols. Paris, 1888–1914.
Ganshof, F. L. "Note sur le sens de 'Ligeris' au titre XLVII de la loi salique en dans le 'Querolus.' " In *Historical Essays in Honor of James Tait*, pp. 111–120. Manchester, 1933.
————. "Note sur les origines de l'union du bénéfice avec vasalité." In *Etudes d'histoire dediée à la mémoire de Henri Pirenne*, pp. 173–189. Brussels, 1937.
————. *Feudalism*. Trans. P. Grierson. London, 1952.
————. "A propos de la cavalrie dans les armées de Charlemagne," *CRAI* (1952), 531–537.
————. "L'Origine des rapports féodo-vassaliques," *I problemi della civilita carolingia: Settimane di studio del Centro Italiano di Studi sull' Alto Medioeveo*, I (1954), 27–53.
Goffart, Walter. *The Le Mans Forgeries: A Chapter from the History of Church Property in the 9th Century*. Cambridge, Mass., 1966.
Grenier, Albert. *Manuel d'archéologie Gallo-Romain*. 5 vols. Paris, 1931–1960.
Gröhler, H. *Über Ursprung und Bedeutung der französischen Ortsnamen*. 2 vols. Heidelberg, 1913–1935.
Grosse, Robert. *Römische Militarsgeschichte vom Gallienus bis zum Beginn der byzantinischen Themenverfassung*. Berlin, 1928.
Guilhiermoz, Paul. *Essai sur l'origine de la noblesse en France au Moyen Age*. Paris, 1902.
Hay, Denis. *Europe: The Emergence of an Idea*. Edinburgh, 1957.
Hodgkin, Thomas. *Italy and Her Invaders*. 8 vols. London, 1880–1899.
Hollister, C. W. *Anglo-Saxon Military Institutions*. Oxford, 1962.
Hoyt, R. S. *Europe in the Middle Ages*. 2nd ed. New York, 1966.
Jones, A. H. M. *The Later Roman Empire*. 2 vols. Norman, Okla., 1964.
Jullian, C. *Histoire de la Gaule Romaine*, vol. VIII. Paris, 1926.
Kroell, Maurice. "Étude sur l'institution des Lites en franc." In *Etudes d'histoire juridiques offertes à Paul Frédéric Girard*, vol. II, pp. 125–208. Paris, 1913.
Kurth, G. *Histoire poétique des Mérovingiens*. Paris, 1893.
————. *Clovis*. 2 vols. 2nd ed. Paris, 1901.
————. *Etudes franques*. 2 vols. Paris, 1919.
Latouche, Robert. *The Birth of the Western Economy*. London, 1961.
Lecointre, J. L. "La Bataille de Poitiers entre Charles Martel et les Sarasins: l'Histoire et la légende; origine de celle-ci," *Bulletin de la Société des Antiquaires de l'Ouest*, 3rd ser., VII (1924), 632–642.
Leighton, Albert. "Early Medieval Transport." Ph.D. dissertation, Berkeley, 1964.
Lesne, E. *La Propriété ecclésiastique en France*. 6 vols. Paris, 1910–1943.
Lévi-Provençal, É. *Histoire de l'espagne musulmane*. 3 vols. Paris, 1950.
Levillain, L., and C. Samaran. "Sur le lieu et la date de la bataille de Poitiers en 732," *BEC*, XCIX (1938). 243–267.

_____. "Campus Martius," *BEC*, CVII (1947–1948), 62–68.

Lewis, A. R. *Emerging Medieval Europe, A.D. 400–1000.* New York, 1967.

Liebmann, R. *Der Untergang des thuringischen Königsreichs in den Jahren 531–5.* Meiningen, 1911.

Lindenschmidt, Ludwig. *Handbuch der deutsche Altertumskunde.* Braunschweig, 1880–1890.

Longnon, A. *Géographie de la Gaule au VIᵉ siècle.* Paris, 1878.

_____. *Les noms de lieu de la France.* Paris, 1920.

Lot, Ferdinand. "Les migrations saxonnes," *RH*, CXIX (1915), 1–40.

_____. *L'Impôt foncier et la capitation personelle.* Paris, 1928.

_____. "La conquête du pays d'entre Seine-et-Loire par les Francs," *RH*, CLXV (1930), 241–253.

_____. *The End of the Ancient World and the Beginnings of the Middle Ages.* Trans. P. M. Mariette. New York, 1931.

_____. "Origine et nature du bénéfice," *Anuario de Historia del Derecho Español*, X (1933), 175–185.

_____. "Les limites de la Sapaudia," *Révue savoisienne*, LXXVII (1935), 146–156.

_____. "La 'Notitia Dignitatum utriusque Imperii . . . ,'" *REA*, XXXVIII (1936), 285–338.

_____. "La victoire sur les Alamans et la conversion de Clovis," *RBPH*, XVII (1938), 63–69.

_____. *L'Art militaire et les armées au moyen âge en Europe et dans proche orient.* 2 vols. Paris, 1946.

_____, C. Pfister, and F. L. Ganshof. *Les destinées de l'empire en Occident de 395 à 888.* 2nd ed. Paris, 1940.

MacMullen, Ramsey. *Soldiers and Civilians in the Later Roman Empire.* Cambridge, Mass., 1963.

Mangoldt-Gaudlitz, Hans von. *Die Reiterei in den germanischen und fränkischen Heeren bis zum Ausgang der deutschen Karolinger.* Berlin, 1922.

Mercier, E. "La Bataille de Poitiers et les vraies causes du recul de l'invasion arabe," *RH*, VII (1878). 1–13.

Mercier, M., and A. Seguin. *Charles Martel et la Bataille de Poitiers.* Paris, 1944.

Mitteis, Heinrich. *Lehnrecht und Staatsgewalt.* Weimar, 1958.

Musset, Lucien. *Les invasiones.* 2nd ed. Paris, 1969.

Niemeyer, J. F. *Mediae Latinitatis Lexicon Minus.* Leiden, 1963.

Odegaard, Charles. *Vassi and Fideles in the Carolingian Empire.* Cambridge, Mass., 1945.

Oman, Charles. *The Art of War in the Middle Ages.* Oxford, 1885.

_____. *The Art of War in the Middle Ages.* Oxford, 1898.

_____. *History of the Art of War in the Middle Ages.* 2 vols. London, 1923.

O'Rahilly, Thomas F. *Early Irish History and Mythology.* Dublin, 1946.

Paribeni, R. "Le dimore dei potentiores ne basso impero," *Mitteilungen des deutschen archäologischen Instituts*, LV (1940), 131–148.

Peucker, Eduard von. *Das deutsche Kriegswesen.* 2 vols. Berlin, 1860–1864.

Pirenne, H. "Le fisc royal de Tournai." In *Mélanges d'histoire du moyen âge offerts à M. Ferdinand Lot.* Paris, 1925.

Planitz, Hans. "Die Scharmannen von Prüm." In *Festschrift für Heinrich Lehmann*, pp. 55–69. Berlin, 1937.

Postan, M., ed. *Cambridge Economic History*, vol. I. 2nd ed. Cambridge, 1966.

BIBLIOGRAPHY

Roloff, Gustav. "Die Umwandlung des fränkischen Heers von Chlodowig bis Karl den Grossen," *Neue Jahrbücher für das klassische Altertum*, IX (1902), 389–399.

Roth, Paul. *Geschichte des Beneficialwesens von ältesten Zeiten bis ins zehnte Jahrhundert.* Erlangen, 1850.

————. *Feudalität und Unterthanverband.* Weimar, 1863.

Rouche, Michel. "Les Aquitans ont-ils trahi avant la Bataille de Poitiers?" *MA*, LXXIV (1968), 5–26.

Roy, Jean-Henri, and Jean Devoisse. *La Bataille de Poitiers.* Paris, 1966.

Rübel, Karl. "Frankisches und spätrömisches Kriegswesen," *Bonner Jahrbücher*, CXIV (1906), 136–142.

Russell, Jeffrey. *Medieval Civilization.* New York, 1968.

Salin, Edouard. *La Civilisation mérovingienne.* 4 vols. Paris, 1949–1959.

Sanchez-Albornoz, Claudio. *En torno a las Orígenes del Feudalismo.* 3 vols. Mendoza, 1942.

Sawyer, Peter. *The Age of the Vikings.* London, 1962.

————, and R. Hilton. "Technical Determinism: The Strirrup and the Plough," *Past and Present*, XXIV (1963), 90–100.

Schmidt, Ludwig. *Geschichte der deutschen Stämme bis zum ausgange der völkerwanderung.* 8 vols. Berlin, 1904–1908.

Seeck, Otto, "Das deutsche Gefolgswesen auf römischen Boden," *ZRG*, XVII (1896), 97–119.

Sprandel, Rolf. "Dux et Comes in der Merowingerzeit," *ZRG*, LXXIV (1957), 41–84.

————. "Bemerkungen zum frühfrankischen Comitat," *ZRG*, LXXXII (1965), 288–291.

Stein, Ernst. "Die Organisation der weströmischen Grenzeverteidigung im V. Jahrhundert und das Burgunderreich am Rhein," *Bericht des deutsches archäologisches Institut, Rom.-Germ. Komm.*, XVIII (1928), 92–114.

————. *Histoire du Bas-Empire.* 2 vols. Paris, 1949–1959.

Stein, F. *Adelsgräber des achten Jahrhundert in Deutschland.* 2 vols. Berlin, 1967.

Stein, S. "Der *Romanus* in des frankischen Rechtsquellen (Eine Antwort)," *Historische Vierteljahrschrift*, XXXI (1936), 232–250.

Stephenson, Carl. "The Origin and Significance of Feudalism," *AHR*, XLVI (1941), 788–812.

Stevens, C. E. *Sidonius Apollinaris and His Age.* Oxford, 1933.

Strayer, Joseph. "The Two Levels of Feudalism." In *Life and Thought in the Middle Ages.* Ed. Robert Hoyt. Minneapolis, 1967.

Stroheker, K. F. *Der senatorische Adel in spätantiken Gallien.* Tübingen, 1946.

Taylor, Charles. "Note on the Origin of the Polyptych." In *Mélanges d'histoire offerts à Henri Pirenne*, vol. II, pp. 475–482. Brussels, 1926.

Tessier, Georges, *Le baptême de Clovis.* Paris, 1964.

Thompson, E. A. "The Settlement of Barbarians in Southern Gaul," *JRS*, XLVI (1956), 65–75.

————. "The Barbarian Kingdoms in Gaul and Spain," *Nottingham Medieval Studies*, VII (1963), 3–33.

————. *The Early Germans.* Oxford, 1965.

————. *The Goths in Spain*, Oxford, 1969.

Van de Vyver, André. "La victoire contre les Alamans et la conversion de Clovis," *RBPH*, XV and XVI (1936 and 1937), 859–914 and 35–94.

_____. "Clovis et la Politique méditerranienne." In *Etudes d'histoire dediée à la mémoire de Henri Pirenne*, pp. 367–388. Brussels, 1937.

_____. "L'unique victoire contre les Alamans et la conversion de Clovis en 506," *RBPH*, XVII (1939), 793–813.

_____. "La chronologie du règne de Clovis d'après la légende et d'après l'histoire," *MA*, LIII (1947), 177–196.

Veeck, W. *Die Alamannen in Württemberg.* 2 vols. Berlin, 1931.

Verbruggen, J. F. *De Krijgskunst in West-Europa in den Middeleeuwen.* Brussels, 1954.

_____. "L'Armée et la stratégie de Charlemagne." In *Karl der Grosse*, vol. I, pp. 420–436. Dusseldorf, 1965.

Vercauteren, F. "Comment s'est-on défendu au IX⁰ siècle dans l'empire franc contre les invasiones normandes?" *XXX⁰ congrès de la Fédération archéologique et historique de Belgique*, pp. 117–132. Brussels, 1935.

Verlinden, Charles. *Les origines de la frontière linguistique en Belgique et la colonisation franque.* Brussels, 1955.

Voltini, H. "Prekarie und Beneficium," *Vierteljahrschrift für Sozial und Wirtschaftsgeschichte*, XVI (1923), 293–305.

Waitz, Georg. *Über die Anfänge der Vassalität.* Göttingen, 1856.

_____. *Deutsche Verfassungsgeschichte.* 8 vols. Berlin, 1874–1885.

Wallace-Hadrill, J. M. *The Fourth Book of the Chronicle of Fredegar.* London, 1960.

_____. *The Long-Haired Kings.* London, 1962.

Werner, Joachim. "Zur Entstehung der Reihengräberzivilisation," *Archaeologia Geographia*, I (1950), 23–32.

_____. "Bewaffnung und Waffenbeigabe in der Merowingerzeit," *Ordinamenti Militari in Occidente nell 'Alto Medioevo (Settimane di Studio del Centro Italiano di Studi sull 'Alto Medioevo*, XV [Spoleto, 1968]), I, 95–108.

White, Lynn, Jr. *Medieval Technology and Social Change.* Oxford, 1962.

Wolfram, Herwig. *Intitulatio I: Lateinische Königs- und Fürstentitel bis zum Ende des 8. Jahrhunderts*, *MIÖG*, Ergänzungband XXI, 1967.

Zöllner, Erich. *Geschichte der Franken.* Munich, 1970.

Index

Index

INDEX

INDEX

Milites, 25, 33–34, 41, 50–51, 62, 71–73, 78–80, 88–89, 108, 124
Milituniae, 79
Minor populus, 55–56, 71
Mummolus, patrician, 38–41, 44, 47, 54–55, 59, 67
Munderic, Frankish magnate, 20–21, 29
Muslims, 101–102, 118

Naix, 82
Nantes, 11, 64, 78–79. *See also* Levies
Narbonne, 101, 105
Narses, 27
Naval forces, 4, 18–20, 34, 38, 89, 108, 111, 128
Neustria, 66, 69, 74, 77, 83, 85, 97
Nevers, 67, 78
Nicetius, Duke, 62, 67
Nîmes, 61, 62, 101
Nobiliores, 87
Notitia Dignitatum, 14, 21

Odilo, Bavarian Duke, 106–107
Olo, Duke, 60
Orange, 62
Orléans, 10, 77–78. *See also* Levies
Ostrogoths, 12, 131
Otto, Frankish magnate, 92

Paris, 4–5, 17, 29, 51, 53, 75, 77–79, 127
Pauperes, 64, 71, 125–126
Peppin I, 92
Peppin II, 97–98, 109–110
Peppin III, 101, 108–111, 122, 126
Périgueux, 53, 57, 85. *See also* Levies
Pisaurum, battle of, 27
Poitiers, 11, 28, 38–39, 42, 49–51, 57–58, 67, 112: battle of, 117; Church of St. Hilary at, 49–50, 101. *See also* Levies
Potentiores, 126
Praetextatus, Bishop of Rouen, 48
Procopius, 26, 79, 113–114: on Frankish warfare, 131–136; evaluation of, 137–138
Protadius, mayor of the palace, 77
Pueri, 32, 38, 46, 50–52, 57, 64–65, 72–73, 85, 97, 99, 124
Pussy, 79

Quintianus, Bishop of Rodez, 7

Rabanus Maurus, 136
Radbod, Duke of Frisia, 99–100
Radulf, Duke of Thuringia, 92–94, 109
Ragamfred, mayor of the palace, 99–101
Ragamund, magnate, 78
Ragnachar, 4, 9, 13, 90
Ragnovald, Duke, 53
Rauching, Duke, 65, 72
Reccared, King of the Visigoths, 61–62
Reguli, 3, 6, 8, 10, 13, 24
Remigius, Bishop of Rheims, 7–8, 14
Rennes, 10
Rheims, 5, 29, 36, 55, 75
Riccar, 13
Rignomer, 13
Rigunth, 57
Ripuarian Franks, 137
Ripuarian Law, 115, 137
Roccolen, Count, 46
Rodan, Lombard Duke, 40
Rodez, 11–12
Roman soldiers, 3, 10
Romani, 79, 106, 111
Romania, 128
Rouen, 46

Sagittarius, Bishop of Gap, 60
St. Boniface, 98
Saint-Moré, 5
Saintes, 12, 47, 85. *See also* Levies
Saintois, 93, 109, 125. *See also* Levies
Salmaise, 34
Samh, -al, 101
Samo, 86
Saragossa, 26, 86
Sarmatians, 5, 12, 17, 34
Satellites, 99, 104
Saxons, 15, 28–29, 32, 36, 41, 82–87, 101, 105, 108, 124, 127: of Bayeux, 10, 15, 52, 63, 71; in Italy, 39
Scapthar, magnate, 28
Scara, 81, 87–88, 109
Scarfa, 78
Seltz, 81
Seniores, 87
Senlis, 5
Septimania, 12, 61, 63, 68, 71

INDEX